DATE DUE

BC-3

CY-5

CHARLES EASTMAN

CHARLES EASTMAN

Sioux Physician and Author

▼ ▼ ▼

Karin Luisa Badt

Senior Consulting Editor
W. David Baird
Howard A. White Professor of History
Pepperdine University

CHELSEA HOUSE PUBLISHERS

New York   Philadelphia

FRONTISPIECE   Charles Eastman, seen here at his 1887 graduation from Dartmouth College in Hanover, New Hampshire, was born on a Santee Sioux reservation near Redwood Falls, Minnesota, in 1858.

ON THE COVER   Eastman appeared as comfortable in a tuxedo as he did in buckskins and a warbonnet. Although he moved easily in the world of the white establishment, the celebrated physician never lost sight of his Native American roots.

Chelsea House Publishers
EDITORIAL DIRECTOR   Richard Rennert
EXECUTIVE MANAGING EDITOR   Karyn Gullen Browne
COPY CHIEF   Robin James
PICTURE EDITOR   Adrian G. Allen
CREATIVE DIRECTOR   Robert Mitchell
ART DIRECTOR   Joan Ferrigno
PRODUCTION MANAGER   Sallye Scott

North American Indians of Achievement
SENIOR EDITOR   Marian W. Taylor
NATIVE AMERICAN SPECIALIST   Jack Miller

Staff for CHARLES EASTMAN
ASSISTANT EDITOR   Margaret Dornfeld
EDITORIAL ASSISTANT   Sydra Mallery
DESIGNER   Lydia Rivera
PICTURE RESEARCHER   Ellen Barrett Dudley
COVER ILLUSTRATOR   Shelly Pritchett

Printed and bound in Mexico.

First Printing

1 3 5 7 9 8 6 4 2

Library of Congress Cataloging-in-Publication Data

Badt, Karin Luisa.
Charles Eastman: Sioux physician and author / Karin Luisa Badt; senior consulting editor, W. David Baird.
  p. cm.—(North American Indians of achievement)
Includes bibliographical references and index.
ISBN 0-7910-2048-7
ISBN 0-7910-2049-5 (pbk.)
1. Eastman, Charles Alexander, 1858–1939—Juvenile literature. 2. Santee Indians— Biography—Juvenile literature. 3. Physicians—United States—Biography—Juvenile litera- ture. [Eastman, Charles Alexander, 1858–1939. 2. Santee Indians—Biography. 3. Indians of North America—Great Plians—Biography.] I.Baird, W. David. II. Title. III. Series.
E99.S22E1847 1995   94-34896
973'.04975'0092—dc20   CIP
[B]   AC

AUG - - 1995

CONTENTS

NORTH AMERICAN INDIANS OF ACHIEVEMENT

BLACK HAWK
Sac Rebel

JOSEPH BRANT
Mohawk Chief

BEN NIGHTHORSE CAMPBELL
Cheyenne Chief and U.S. Senator

COCHISE
Apache Chief

CRAZY HORSE
Sioux War Chief

CHARLES EASTMAN
Sioux Physician and Author

CHIEF GALL
Sioux War Chief

GERONIMO
Apache Warrior

HIAWATHA
Founder of the
Iroquois Confederacy

CHIEF JOSEPH
Nez Perce Leader

PETER MACDONALD
Former Chairman of
the Navajo Nation

WILMA MANKILLER
Principal Chief of the Cherokees

OSCEOLA
Seminole Rebel

QUANAH PARKER
Comanche Chief

KING PHILIP
Wampanoag Rebel

POCAHONTAS
Powhatan Peacemaker

PONTIAC
Ottawa Rebel

RED CLOUD
Sioux War Chief

WILL ROGERS
Cherokee Entertainer

SITTING BULL
Chief of the Sioux

TECUMSEH
Shawnee Rebel

JIM THORPE
Sac and Fox Athlete

SARAH WINNEMUCCA
Northern Paiute Writer and Diplomat

Other titles in preparation

ON INDIAN LEADERSHIP

by W. David Baird
Howard A. White Professor of History
Pepperdine University

Authoritative utterance is in thy mouth, perception is in thy heart, and thy tongue is the shrine of justice," the ancient Egyptians said of their king. From him, the Egyptians expected authority, discretion, and just behavior. Homer's *Iliad* suggests that the Greeks demanded somewhat different qualities from their leaders: justice and judgment, wisdom and counsel, shrewdness and cunning, valor and action. It is not surprising that different people living at different times should seek different qualities from the individuals they looked to for guidance. By and large, a people's requirements for leadership are determined by two factors: their culture and the unique circumstances of the time and place in which they live.

Before the late 15th century, when non-Indians first journeyed to what is now North America, most Indian tribes were not ruled by a single person. Instead, there were village chiefs, clan headmen, peace chiefs, war chiefs, and a host of other types of leaders, each with his or her own specific duties. These influential people not only decided political matters but also helped shape their tribe's social, cultural, and religious life. Usually, Indian leaders held their positions because they had won the respect of their peers. Indeed, if a leader's followers at any time decided that he or she was out of step with the will of the people, they felt free to look to someone else for advice and direction.

Thus, the greatest achievers in traditional Indian communities were men and women of extraordinary talent. They were not only skilled at navigating the deadly waters of tribal politics and cultural customs but also able to, directly or indirectly, make a positive and significant difference in the daily life of their followers.

From the beginning of their interaction with Native Americans, non-Indians failed to understand these features of Indian leadership. Early European explorers and settlers merely assumed that Indians had the same relationship with their leaders as non-Indians had with their kings and queens. European monarchs generally inherited their positions and ruled large nations however they chose, often with little regard for the desires or needs of their subjects. As a result, the settlers of Jamestown saw Pocahontas as a "princess" and Pilgrims dubbed Wampanoag leader Metacom "King Philip," envisioning them in roles very different from those in which their own people placed them.

As more and more non-Indians flocked to North America, the nature of Indian leadership gradually began to change. Influential Indians no longer had to take on the often considerable burden of pleasing only their own people; they also had to develop a strategy of dealing with the non-Indian newcomers. In a rapidly changing world, new types of Indian role models with new ideas and talents continually emerged. Some were warriors; others were peacemakers. Some held political positions within their tribes; others were writers, artists, religious prophets, or athletes. Although the demands of Indian leadership altered from generation to generation, several factors that determined which Indian people became prominent in the centuries after first contact remained the same.

Certain personal characteristics distinguished these Indians of achievement. They were intelligent, imaginative, practical, daring, shrewd, uncompromising, ruthless, and logical. They were constant in friendships, unrelenting in hatreds, affectionate with their relatives, and respectful to their God or gods. Of course, no single Native American leader embodied all these qualities, nor these qualities only. But it was these characteristics that allowed them to succeed.

The special skills and talents that certain Indians possessed also brought them to positions of importance. The life of Hiawatha, the legendary founder of the powerful Iroquois Confederacy, displays the value that oratorical ability had for many Indians in power.

The biography of Cochise, the 19th-century Apache chief, illustrates that leadership often required keen diplomatic skills not only in transactions among tribespeople but also in hardheaded negotiations with non-Indians. For others, such as Mohawk Joseph Brant and Navajo Peter MacDonald, a non-Indian education proved advantageous in their dealings with other peoples.

Sudden changes in circumstance were another crucial factor in determining who became influential in Indian communities. King Philip in the 1670s and Geronimo in the 1880s both came to power when their people were searching for someone to lead them into battle against white frontiersmen who had forced upon them a long series of indignities. Seeing the rising discontent of Indians of many tribes in the 1810s, Tecumseh and his brother, the Shawnee prophet Tenskwatawa, proclaimed a message of cultural revitalization that appealed to thousands. Other Indian achievers recognized cooperation with non-Indians as the most advantageous path during their lifetime. Sarah Winnemucca in the late 19th century bridged the gap of understanding between her people and their non-Indian neighbors through the publication of her autobiography *Life Among the Piutes*. Olympian Jim Thorpe in the early 20th century championed the assimilationist policies of the U.S. government and, with his own successes, demonstrated the accomplishments Indians could make in the non-Indian world. And Wilma Mankiller, principal chief of the Cherokees, continues to fight successfully for the rights of her people through the courts and through negotiation with federal officials.

Leadership among Native Americans, just as among all other peoples, can be understood only in the context of culture and history. But the centuries that Indians have had to cope with invasions of foreigners in their homelands have brought unique hardships and obstacles to the Native American individuals who most influenced and inspired others. Despite these challenges, there has never been a lack of Indian men and women equal to these tasks. With such strong leaders, it is no wonder that Native Americans remain such a vital part of this nation's cultural landscape.

1

THE BATTLE OF WOUNDED KNEE

An officer of the 9th U.S. cavalry surveys the aftermath of the December 29, 1890, struggle at Wounded Knee, South Dakota. Perceiving the event as a massacre rather than a battle, Charles Eastman began to doubt the humanity of white Americans.

Dr. Charles Eastman would never forget the horror of December 29, 1890.

Eastman had expected to spend the evening relaxing after a day of visiting his patients at the Pine Ridge reservation in South Dakota. Instead, he was called that evening to the Pine Ridge chapel to handle an emergency. A battle had broken out between the Sioux American Indians and the United States Army's Seventh Cavalry. More than 150 Sioux had been slaughtered, and the few who survived were badly wounded.

Eastman was the only doctor in the area. He had very little experience behind him, having just graduated that June from the Boston University School of Medicine. Still, he was determined to do his best. As the government doctor for the Pine Ridge Indian Agency, he would take on the responsibility of mending the torn and mutilated bodies that filled the chapel.

For weeks, Eastman had been afraid that something terrible might happen. That November when he arrived on the reservation, he noticed that tensions were high between the Sioux and the U.S. government. The federal government had been making many efforts to encourage the Sioux to adopt, as quickly as possible, the customs of white society. It decided that the best way to do so would be to force the Sioux to abandon their traditional ways—something the Native Americans were reluctant to do. The Sioux were nomadic hunters who, for centuries, had roamed freely in the open prairies of the Northwest. How could a people accustomed to this way of life be persuaded to assume the American values of private land ownership and individualism?

The U.S. government thought the answer lay in persuading the Sioux to become farmers and herdsmen. If each Indian farmed his own private lot of land, he might soon give up his feelings of being part of a group in which everything was shared. The federal government's hope was that the Indians would eventually become peaceful, law-abiding residents—if not full citizens—of the United States. After all, the Native American tribes had to be dealt with if American settlers were to claim the West for themselves.

The U.S. government was aggressive in its efforts to erase the Indians' traditional way of life. The federal government introduced herds of cattle and crop farming to the Great Sioux reservation in Dakota. Then, in April 1888, the government decided to divide the reservation into six smaller reservations. This division was yet another step to force the Sioux to stop thinking of themselves as a united people. Moreover, in dividing the reservation, the U.S. government managed to take 11 million acres of the best land for itself.

An Arapaho man takes part in the Ghost Dance in 1893. The U.S. government sought to suppress the Ghost Dance religion, which frightened whites with its promise that the earth would one day be free of white people.

The results of these efforts were disastrous. In 1888, the herds of cattle were ravaged by disease. In 1889, the crops failed. Epidemics of influenza, measles, and whooping cough decimated the Indian camps. The surviving Sioux were reduced to being dependent on food rations from the federal government. They felt cheated and angry. How, on the grassy plains of South Dakota, could they be expected to become like the successful farmers working the rich soil of Ohio and Pennsylvania? The Native Americans recognized that they had lost in every dealing they had with the federal government.

Around this time, a Paiute holy man from Nevada named Wovoka began preaching a strange new religion, called the Ghost Dance. Wovoka prophesied that if the Indians performed certain rites and dances, a great flood would drench the earth and drown the white people. After the flood, the land would once again be the domain of the Indians, who would be united as one people. New soil would cover the continent and bury the white men. The

Wovoka (left), pictured with an actor in 1926, founded the Ghost Dance religion after having a vision of a renewed world. Many Native Americans were eager to accept his teachings, which offered hope of recovering their lost land and reversing the destruction of their culture.

ghosts of dead Indians would then join the living Indians in this paradise, and together they would live peacefully on the regenerated land. It was a fantastic vision, and to many Native Americans, it offered the only hope they had that they were not doomed to extinction, which seemed very likely at the time.

The Ghost Dance religion spread like wildfire. Demoralized, hungry, and embittered by their situation, thousands of Indians were drawn to the new religion and its promises. Chiefs from different tribes traveled to learn the prophet's dance and then taught it to their people. Within the span of just two years—January 1889 to November 1890—the Ghost Dance religion spread throughout the interior West, from western Nevada to Missouri.

The U.S. government objected to the new religion. Although the Ghost Dance was a peaceful activity, it frightened the whites because of its inflammatory message. Who knew where the dance would lead? One white man, Dr. Daniel Royer, the newly appointed Indian agent at the Pine Ridge reservation, was so terrified that he wrote many nervous letters to the federal government in Washington, D.C., begging for troops to come and make the Native Americans stop dancing. "Indians are dancing in the snow and are wild and crazy," he wrote in one particularly frantic telegram on November 15, 1890. "We need protection and we need it now."

On December 14, Indian police were ordered to arrest Sitting Bull, a leader in the Ghost Dance movement. Sitting Bull put up no fight when the police came to his camp and told him he had to turn himself in. Because he had just awakened, he asked for some time to put on his clothes. All of a sudden, one of Sitting Bull's men pulled out a rifle and shot at the Indian police. A skirmish broke out, and Sitting Bull, who had barely woken up, was shot in the head.

Sitting Bull's people, the Sioux Hunkpapas, fled the camp, afraid for their lives. A hundred of them joined the camp of another chief, Big Foot, and his people. That same day, the U.S. government's Department of War issued orders for Big Foot's arrest. He was considered a dangerous leader in the Ghost Dance movement. The reality was that Big Foot had recently become disillusioned with the Ghost Dance religion and no longer firmly believed in the vision of the Paiute prophet.

When Big Foot heard that Sitting Bull had been killed, he decided to move his men to the Pine Ridge reservation, where he hoped to ask another chief, Red Cloud, for protection. It was a cold, long walk in the snow to Pine Ridge. On the way, Big Foot contracted pneumonia.

Meanwhile, the U.S. Army sent five companies of infantry and three companies of calvary to pursue Big Foot and his people. One of these troops, the Seventh Cavalry, met Big Foot near Porcupine Creek, a short distance from the reservation. Big Foot had no intention of fighting and ordered that a white flag of surrender be run up over his wagon. He sat up in his blankets, coughing, to greet Major Samuel Whitside. Someone later reported that as Big Foot spoke, blood sputtered from his nose and mouth while he shivered in the bitter cold.

Whitside announced that his orders were to confiscate the Indians' weapons. He insisted that Big Foot and his people move on to a new camp, at Wounded Knee, where the cavalry was based. Barely able to sit up, Big Foot was quiet as he looked at the military men, with their guns gleaming from the glare of the snow. He had no choice but to agree.

The next morning, after receiving their breakfast rations, the Native Americans were told to pile up their guns in front of the soldiers. Reluctantly, the warriors dropped one rifle after another in front of the soldiers, 40 in all. Still, the soldiers were not satisfied. They ransacked the tents and ripped apart the Indians' belongings. The soldiers took the Indians' axes, knives, and even tent stakes and piled them on top of the guns.

Neither the Indians nor the soldiers thought that any violence would break out. It was obvious to both sides that the Native Americans were outnumbered: there were 500 soldiers and only 350 Indians, more than half of whom were women and children. Nevertheless, the confiscating of the guns increased the Indians' feelings of resentment. As the soldiers harassed the Native Ameri-

A troop of Indian police stands at attention in the 1890s. The law enforcement unit, made up of Native Americans loyal to the U.S. government, was responsible for maintaining order on reservations.

cans and demanded their weapons, a medicine man named Yellow Bird began to dance and blow on an eagle-bone whistle, trying to incite the men to rebel.

One deaf Indian refused to give up his gun. Most likely he did not hear the order. In any event, a soldier grabbed him and wrestled with the gun, angry at the Indian's stubbornness. A shot rang out, and the Battle of Wounded Knee had begun. The U.S. Army proceeded to fire at men, women, and children. Native American warriors fought back with the clubs and knives they had been hiding under their blankets. A murderous fight ensued, as the soldiers and Indians shot, stabbed, and clubbed each other, giving vent to the tensions that had been building up since the night before. Big Foot sat up to watch from his stretcher and was met with a volley of bullets.

Yellow Bird had said that the ghost shirts the Indians were wearing would protect them from the white man's

The chapel at South Dakota's Pine Ridge reservation served as a hospital after the Wounded Knee massacre. Tending the injured there, Charles Eastman found himself overwhelmed by the extent of his people's suffering.

guns, but this certainly did not turn out to be the case. Within just a few minutes, the bodies of more than half of the Indians had been laced with bullets.

The warriors were the first to be shot down. The women and children of the camp, who had gathered by their tepees to watch the battle, were mowed down with bullets from the cavalry's powerful Hotchkiss gun. One woman, Blue Whirlwind, received 14 wounds, while her two sons at her side were also shot. By then, the ground was littered with the corpses of more than 150 Indians and 25 U.S. soldiers. Smoke rose from the camp as some of the tepees, ripped apart by bullets, became engulfed in flames.

The surviving Indians panicked and tried to escape toward a ravine, but they were pursued by hundreds of maddened soldiers. What had begun as a battle between two sides had turned quickly into a massacre of unarmed people. Soldiers shot at everybody who moved: women with infants in their arms, small children crawling toward the woods, the few remaining warriors.

After the battle had died down, the wounded soldiers were taken to the army field hospital, while most of the wounded Sioux were brought to a chapel that had been converted into a hospital. To make more space in the chapel, a Christmas tree adorned with ornaments had been pushed behind the altar. It was in this chapel that 32-year-old Charles Eastman worked through the night, trying to save dozens of the wounded Indians.

"We tore out the pews," Eastman later wrote about that evening, "and covered the floor with hay and quilts. There we laid the poor creatures side by side in rows, and the night was devoted to caring for them as best we could. The suffering was terrible." He recalled in particular one young girl who screamed for the doctor to take off her ghost shirt, which had become torn and spotted with her own blood.

The complexity of Eastman's reactions to the sight of slaughter cannot be underestimated. In his youth he was Ohiyesa, a Santee Sioux, destined to become a warrior like his father, and yet, there he was in 1890, working for the U.S. Indian Agency to save his people, using skills he had just learned as a student at Boston University's Medical School. Whereas the Battle of Wounded Knee marked the clash between two cultures, Charles Eastman represented the merging of those same two cultures.

How Ohiyesa became Dr. Charles Eastman is a story not only of an exceptionally intelligent and profoundly driven man, but of a crucial period in United States history. His life story bears witness to the incredible challenge that faced Native Americans at the turn of the 20th century: to remain true to their traditions and people while accepting the conquest of the white man.

2

"THE FREEST LIFE IN THE WORLD"

Hakadah, later known as Ohiyesa, and then as Charles Eastman, was born into the Santee Sioux tribe on February 19, 1858, near Redwood Falls, Minnesota. Still untouched by white civilization, the deep forest of the boy's birthplace boasted herds of antelope, elk, and deer. Wild rice grew in the lakes and was harvested, when the time came, by Sioux women from their canoes. Hakadah's was a largely tranquil existence, but he later remembered an ever present feeling of adventure in the air. At any time, a person might come across a six-foot grizzly bear or be set upon by a warrior from an enemy tribe.

A century earlier, the Sioux had been a great and powerful people. They were originally from Minnesota, but in the 17th century pressure from the Ojibwa Indians and the French had forced them to move west, where they eventually occupied parts of present-day North and South Dakota, Minnesota, Iowa, and Wisconsin. The Sioux had other reasons, too, for emigrating: the western plains offered a rich new hunting ground; here, buffalo roamed by the million.

During its westward migration, over a period of several hundred years, the Sioux Nation split into three groups: the Western (or Teton) Sioux, the Northern (Yankton) Sioux, and the Eastern (Santee) Sioux. Each division developed its own distinct lifestyle. The Teton Sioux, for example, became nomadic buffalo hunters on the flat plains of present-day South Dakota and Wyoming. They moved often, changing camp as they conquered new territory from their enemies, and as the buffalo moved from one feeding ground to another.

Eastman's people, the Santee Sioux, lived in the forests of Minnesota. Like the Tetons, they hunted, but they also practiced rudimentary agriculture. In the summer, they gathered wild rice and harvested their crops of sweet potatoes, turnips, and corn, and in the spring, the old people, women, and children boiled birch-tree sap for sugar. Somewhat more peaceful than their Teton relatives, the Santee nevertheless took part in almost constant warfare, attacking other tribes to avenge the death of a relative, acquire new territory, or capture horses.

Each division of the Sioux nation boasted as many as seven distinct bands—each band consisting of a group of *tiyospayes.* The basic unit of Sioux society, the tiyospaye was an extended family that included grandparents, parents, children, uncles, aunts, and cousins. Sometimes, during the winter months especially, a tiyospaye would separate from the band to fare for itself. In a hunting economy, people must disperse every so often because the food supply in one place is rarely adequate. The separated tiyospayes would rejoin the band after their independent hunting expeditions.

Leading each tiyospaye was a man chosen for his possession of the four great virtues in Sioux culture:

An Eastman canvas depicts a Sioux family preparing to break camp. Pursuing their ever-moving quarry, the Sioux traveled from one location to another during hunting season.

bravery, fortitude, generosity, and wisdom. If a leader also proved himself an outstanding hunter or warrior, he could aspire to an even higher position of tribal political power: that of Shirt Wearer (spokesman of the tribe), Pipe Bearer (counselor), Whip Bearer (policeman), or, if he was particularly gifted, chief. Sioux society treated its leaders with great respect and honor.

Hakadah came from a long line of leaders. His father, Ikee Wakandhi (Many Lightnings), was the chief of his band, as his father had been before him. Hakadah's mother, Wakantankwanwin (Goddess), was the granddaughter of Mahpiya Wichasta, Chief Cloud Man. Hakadah's noble line of ancestors was an important part of his life; in the Sioux culture, the child of

prestigious parents was expected to equal them and to cast honor on their memory.

Wakantankwanwin did cast honor on the memory of her grandfather, the renowned Chief Cloud Man. She impressed whites and Indians alike with what one observer called "beauty of body and soul." In a 1920 letter, E. J. Pond, the son of a missionary who worked with the Mdewakanton band, wrote about Wakantankwanwin in glowing terms. Not only was she "prepossessing in appearance," he said, she was "as bright and intelligent as she was handsome." Her name, "Goddess," was one that no other Sioux woman had ever been given. Hakadah never knew his mother, who died at the age of 28, shortly after giving birth to him. It was this misfor-

A party of Sioux sets out on a hunting expedition in a painting by Seth Eastman. Because few regions supplied enough game to support an entire band, tiyospayes, or extended families, often hunted separately.

tune that gave him has name: Hakadah means "the Pitiful Last." He would have to prove himself before he could earn a more honorable name.

Despite the loss of his mother, Hakadah enjoyed a secure and protected childhood. He was well cared for by the tiyospaye's other members: his father, his older sister and four older brothers, his uncles and aunts, and his beloved paternal grandmother, Uncheedah. Like other Sioux babies, he traveled strapped to a cradle-board, and his grandmother would hang board and baby on a tree branch, keeping an eye on him as she gathered firewood. At night, she would sing him songs or tell him stories about great warriors and their amazing deeds. Hakadah never cried, but in that he was typical of most Sioux children. Because wailing was likely to indicate the camp's position to enemy tribes, children were trained from birth to make very little noise.

Enemy attacks usually took place at daybreak, so the Sioux rose at dawn. To the children, the day was something to look forward to, and they rarely protested getting up so early. They had only one obligation—to play. For the boys, there were bow-and-arrow competitions, swimming contests, pony races, wrestling matches, lacrosse games, and mud-ball fights. In the winter, the youngsters made ice skates from strips of basswood bark and raced each other on the frozen lakes. Sometimes they raced on sleighs made from buffalo ribs.

For the Sioux children, the outdoors was both playground and school. It was by playing that they learned and prepared for their future roles. The games the boys played emphasized strength, agility, and cunning—skills necessary for a successful hunt or surprise attack on an enemy camp. In one typical game, the boys would paint themselves as warriors and, with a war

cry, attack a nest of bees, pretending they were Ojibwa Indians or some other Sioux enemy.

Sioux children did not worry about what time they had to be back home. Not only was the outdoors home, but Indians did not measure time by hours, minutes, and seconds. Instead, each day followed the rhythm of the sun's movement across the sky. As Eastman later wrote, "It was the freest life in the world."

When Hakadah was still a young boy, he had the chance to earn a new name. The spring fur hunters had been successful, and the maize and potatoes the women had planted were growing well. To celebrate, the different Santee Sioux bands had gathered together for a feast.

Sioux men converge on the ball during a lacrosse game. The young Charles Eastman won the name Ohiyesa (the Winner) after helping his band to a solid lacrosse victory.

There were to be all sorts of athletic events, the most important of which was the lacrosse game. A medicine man announced that Hakadah would represent his band, the Wahpetons, in the game against the Kaposias. If his band won, Hakadah would receive a new name.

It was a suspenseful game as hundreds of Sioux warriors scrambled to catch the ball in their netted sticks, racing across a field that was almost a mile long. The game must have been a spectacular event in the deep quiet of Minnesota. As Eastman later described it, "a hundred lacrosse sticks vied with each other, and the wriggling human flesh and paint were all one could see through the cloud of dust." War whoops echoed far in the forest as the Indians cried out their support for their bands.

The Wahpetons won the lacrosse game. And, as promised, Hakadah was given his new name, a name that heralded his future as one of the most successful Indian men of his time. Hakadah was now Ohiyesa, the Winner.

And yet the year was 1862, a year that would soon be understood as one of the worst in Sioux history. Life as Ohiyesa knew it would soon come to an end.

3

THE SIOUX UPRISING

August 17, 1862, was the day that sealed the fate of the Santee Sioux. That Sunday morning, four young Indians were coming back from a hunting expedition in Acton, Minnesota. They were in low spirits. Not only had the whites cheated them out of much of their land with dubious treaties, but they had disturbed the herds of animals on which the Sioux depended for food. The hunt had gone badly.

Making things worse, the Indians were not sure that the U.S. government would deliver that year's annuity. (The annuity that concerned them was a yearly supply of money and food, paid by the government to the Indians in return for their land and their promise to keep the peace.) The annuity had been promised in July; now it was August, and the Indians had still seen no sign of it. Thousands of Sioux were starving, but white traders, believing that the Indians had been abandoned by the government, were no longer extending credit to them.

Sioux warriors attack a settler family during the Sioux Uprising of 1862. The massacre was triggered by the Sioux's loss of both their land and their means of independent survival.

29

Wending their way home, the four dejected young men passed a neatly kept, prosperous farm. At the edge of a field they spotted a clutch of eggs left to spoil in the sun. Given the stark situation, it is perhaps not surprising that the sight of the eggs left in the grass and the farmer's fat chickens and ripe grain made the hunters angry. They knew the farmer, Robinson Jones, and decided to demand food from him.

For years, Jones had been selling whiskey to the Indians, from whom he made a comfortable side income. Still, he did not seem pleased to see the men at his front door. His wife was not at home, he said brusquely, so he could give them nothing to eat. The Indians shouted at him, but he paid them no attention.

Gathering up his two youngest children, he walked down the road to his son-in-law's house, where his wife was. The Indians followed him. When Jones's son-in-law, Howard Baker, came out to greet the arrivals, the Indians proposed a competitive game of target shooting. Baker must have noticed the tension between them and his father-in-law, but he agreed to the game, perhaps thinking it might help everyone relax. He was wrong.

As Jones's and Baker's wives watched from the door of the house, each of the men fired one round. After that, one of the young Sioux, apparently ready to give bloody expression to the rage he had been building for months, suddenly shot Jones in the head. Then he swung his rifle toward the two women. Baker jumped in front of his wife. She became the only white adult to survive the incident that would be known as the Acton massacre.

The violence did not end with the massacre at Baker's farm. After murdering the Jones family, the four young Sioux went to another settler's house, stole his horses, and

Federal Indian agents (center) prepare to distribute food rations to the Sioux. By the late 19th century, the Santee Sioux had been forced into dependence on government annuities.

galloped off to the Indian Agency, where their band was living. There they intended to propose a wide-ranging rebellion.

The history of the Santee Sioux's relations with white people begins in the 17th century, when French explorers, fur traders, and missionaries first came into Sioux territory. The Indians gained some advantages from this first encounter, acquiring such European goods as guns, horses, metal cooking pots, and tools. Ultimately, however, the arrival of the Europeans spelled deep trouble for the Native Americans: the French brought not only pots and pans but sickness. Soon after their arrival, epidemics began to decimate large numbers of Sioux, who were especially vulnerable to European diseases.

By the mid-1700s, the Santees had learned that another kind of white society had sprung up on the East Coast of the continent. These colonists were said to be expanding

their settlements westward. When the Revolutionary War broke out, the Sioux and other Native American tribes decided to fight alongside the British, believing that if they played one group of white people off against another, they could defend their land from further encroachment. What they did not expect was that the colonists would win the war. A few years later, in 1805, the United States forced the Santees to sign peace treaties in which they lost over 100,000 acres of land.

The War of 1812 gave the Santees new hope. As before, they sided with the British. But the United States won again. And once again, the Santees found themselves in the position of the conquered. The new peace treaties forced the Santees to relinquish all rights to their land in Minnesota and move onto reservations. In exchange for giving up their land, the Sioux were to receive annuities—food and money that would keep them alive. While the United States hoped to eventually clear the

The Minnesota militia fires on Santee Sioux warriors during the Battle of Birch Coulee on September 2, 1862. After their defeat, the Sioux were driven from their Minnesota homelands.

Midwest of Indians, they did not want, at least in policy, the Indians to starve to death.

The Acton massacre can only be understood in the context of this long history of defeat. The Sioux felt cheated. They had lost nearly everything they had, and they had received nothing in return. Or so it seemed. Actually, the overdue annuity money had been delivered just the day before the massacre. But by then it was too late.

On the night of August 17th, the four Indians responsible for the massacre went to tell their story to Little Crow, chief of the Mdewakanton band. When he had

Assembled outside the town of Mankato, Minnesota, on December 26, 1862, a crowd awaits the hanging of the 38 Sioux blamed for the Sioux Uprising. Ohiyesa received word that his father was among those executed.

heard their tale, Little Crow decided the situation did not allow for choices. The whites would be coming for revenge, and he saw no alternative but to continue the battle. Little Crow gave orders to attack the trading post at daybreak and kill the traders.

Thus began the bloody conflict known as the Sioux Uprising. In the first week, the Sioux killed every white man, woman, and child they encountered. Some of the victims had long histories of friendship with the Sioux, but in this war, all whites were the same. The Santee warriors took special vengeance on the outpost traders, greedy men who, in their eagerness to dominate the fur trade, had repeatedly cheated the Sioux hunters. More than one dead trader was found with his mouth stuffed with grass, a symbol of broken promises.

After a week of bloodsoaked victories, the Minnesota militia, led by General Hiram Sibley, arrived on the scene, and the Sioux once again found themselves on the defensive. They lost most of the ensuing skirmishes, and after the Battle of Wood Lake, on September 23, 1862, they admitted defeat. The Sioux Uprising was over.

It was not, of course, forgotten. The settlers wanted revenge for those terrible weeks. For them, it was not enough that the Santees had lost in their last attempt to fight back, nor that many Sioux had opposed the uprising. The settlers demanded that the Sioux be punished, and the government obliged. It tried almost 400 Sioux at a military tribunal, and sentenced 303 of them to die on the gallows. In addition, all Santee Sioux were to be expelled from Minnesota and relocated in Dakota Territory. Treaties that had been made with them, promising reservation land and annuities, were to be cancelled. The Santees had begun the uprising out of misery; now they were at the gates of hell itself.

President Abraham Lincoln recognized the injustice of condemning to death warriors who had fought for what they saw as their tribe's welfare and honor. Despite the political risk of angering the Minnesota settlers, he personally reexamined the records of each of the prisoners, finally reducing the death sentences from 303 to 38. One of the remaining condemned was Ohiyesa's father, Many Lightnings.

4

ESCAPE TO CANADA

Concerned about white reactions to their uprising, many Santee Sioux fled Minnesota. One of them was the young Ohiyesa, who was highly excited by the prospect of traveling in the ox-drawn carts his relatives had borrowed from a friendly farmer. He had never been in a wheeled cart. Up to this point, the only conveyance the boy had seen was the *travois*, a traditional Indian vehicle that consisted of two long poles with a sling between them, which was dragged on the ground by a horse (or, occasionally, by a woman). The travois was useful for carrying cargo or elderly and sick people, but at this point the Sioux could not afford to use it: it was too slow, and General Sibley was after them, determined to rid Minnesota of the people so feared and hated by the settlers.

With Sibley and his troops in hot pursuit, the Sioux dashed up to the bank of the Missouri River. There, working quickly, they constructed a series of small, round vessels faced with buffalo hides. Some of the women

Ohiyesa (pictured in formal tribal regalia) learned the skills of a hunter and warrior from his paternal uncle, Mysterious Medicine. An expert marksman by the age of 15, the young Sioux was prepared to avenge his father's death.

37

swam alongside the buffalo boats, tugging them along against the current. Then, once they crossed the Missouri, the Wahpeton band, led by Ohiyesa's paternal uncle, Mysterious Medicine, continued the long and difficult journey north. Often they did not even stop to sleep or eat, and they sometimes found no food for days on end. Forced to cross enemy territory, they lived in constant fear of an ambush. True to their tradition, the Sioux reacted to these hardships without a word of complaint.

Eventually the Wahpetons settled in Manitoba, Canada. Here their tepees offered scant protection from the

A group of Santee Sioux face the camera in Canada, where they had fled in fear of white revenge for the 1862 rebellion. The exiled Sioux managed to maintain their traditional lifestyle for a short time longer, allowing Ohiyesa to learn the values and knowledge of his ancestors.

subzero temperatures and winds; during blizzards they had to bury themselves in the snow in order to keep warm. Nevertheless, Canada was a welcome exile. The cold was a small price to pay for the chance to enjoy what had become impossible in Minnesota: a traditional Indian life.

The stability of Ohiyesa's family life helped him get past the loss of his father and his homeland. Uncheedah, his grandmother, continued to take care of him, bringing him up as she had his father. Every day she would take him with her in the forest while she gathered roots and berries. At night she would tell him stories about his brave ancestors. As the daughter of a chief, Uncheedah was fiercely proud of her Sioux heritage. That the whites had defeated them in Minnesota was no matter, she told her grandson. He would continue in the ways of his forefathers. He, too, would be a great hunter and warrior.

Uncheedah demonstrated by her own example the virtues she wished her grandson to have: patience, courage, and readiness for self-sacrifice. When Ohiyesa was seven, she, already an old woman, swam across a river with him on her back so he would not have to risk his life in one of the round buffalo boats. Another day, she spotted strange footprints near the camp and ran for a double-barreled shotgun. When five Ojibwa warriors appeared at her tepee, she drove them away with a volley of shots. On still another occasion, a party of Ojibwa surprised the camp while most of the men were out hunting. Boldly approaching them, she offered a handshake, thus forestalling a conflict.

Strong and determined, Uncheedah was also a medicine woman, someone gifted with an exceptional knowledge of the ways of nature. Her powers of observation were so great that other members of the tribe saw her as almost supernatural. Uncheedah shared much of her knowledge with Ohiyesa. She taught him about the different plants in the woods—which ones were good to eat and which made good medicine. It was perhaps Uncheedah's influence that inspired Ohiyesa's later decision to become a doctor for his people.

Uncheedah gave her grandson lessons in all aspects of Sioux culture. She taught him about the Great Mystery—Wankan Tanka, the spirit of creation that controlled the universe. Wankan Tanka, she told him, was expressed everywhere in nature; he was not one god, but many, and it was important to revere and understand his power. The more in touch one was with his power, Uncheedah told Ohiyesa, the more one would feel directed in his or her life. Ohiyesa would spend days by himself in the woods, trying to get closer to Wankan Tanka by silently observing the birds and animals.

As he grew older, Ohiyesa began to spend more time with his uncle, Mysterious Medicine, who treated him as his own son. Every morning he would tell Ohiyesa to look closely at everything he saw, and each evening he would question the boy about what he had learned. "What side of the tree has lighter colored bark?" and "How do you know if there are fish in a lake?" he would ask. A Sioux education required the ability to concentrate and remember, and Ohiyesa did his best to please his uncle. His quick mind and powers of observation made him a good student.

Mysterious Medicine sometimes used harsh methods to teach his nephew. Ohiyesa was often startled in the early morning by his uncle shouting or firing a gun outside his tepee, testing Ohiyesa's ability to respond quickly to danger. Ohiyesa would jump up with his weapon in hand, crying out a traditional war whoop. If he moved slowly, his uncle would ridicule him.

Stampeding buffalo flee Sioux hunters in this 1840 engraving. At that point, great buffalo herds still roamed the plains, but by the time Ohiyesa reached manhood, whites had virtually wiped out the animals.

Mysterious Medicine often brought Ohiyesa along with him on his hunting expeditions, teaching him the ways of the buffalo, deer, and grizzly bear. To strengthen his young nephew's courage, he would ask him to go alone in the woods after dark and find water for the camp. When the boy returned, his uncle would thank him and then empty the pail of water on the ground. Ohiyesa would have to go back a second time. He would do so willingly for, as he later wrote, "I wished to be a brave man as much as a white boy desires to be a great lawyer or even president of the United States."

At the age of eight, Ohiyesa had his first important chance to prove his manhood. As part of the initiation rite to celebrate his passage from childhood, Uncheedah asked him to sacrifice his dearest possession to the Great Mystery. Ohiyesa offered his bear claw necklace or his otterskin headdress, but Uncheedah shook her head. Neither was his most cherished possession. There was something far more important to him: his dog, Ohitika. In responding, Ohiyesa remembered his grandmother's often-repeated adage: "Tears for woman and the war-whoop for man to drown sorrow!" That evening Ohiyesa did as he was instructed and sacrificed his own dog, concluding the ritual, as was the custom, by eating pieces of the cooked meat.

Even at this young age, Ohiyesa demonstrated the inner strength and resolve that would later distinguish him. In any situation, he unflinchingly pursued the path he thought was right. In his approach to life, he exemplified the Sioux virtues of self-discipline and fortitude.

One day, Ohiyesa learned he had a mission: his uncle told him he was to avenge his father's death. No American was to be spared. For an example to follow, Ohiyesa could look to Mysterious Medicine, who crossed the U.S.–Canadian border every summer and returned with white scalps.

By the time he was 14 years old, Ohiyesa had become expert in the skills he had been taught. He went hunting alone now, returning after a long day in the woods with game for the women to cook. He had become adept not only with a bow and arrow, but with a gun. Ohiyesa was ready. As he later put it, "I had now taken part in all our tribal activities except war, and was nearly old enough to be initiated into the ritual of the war-path. The world was full of natural rivalry; I was eager for the day." The time had come when he must prove himself as a warrior, the true son of his father.

This was the path Ohiyesa would probably have followed had an incredible event not changed everything.

5

▼ ▼ ▼

THE RETURN

Returning from a hunting expedition one day in September 1872, 14-year-old Ohiyesa saw a stranger emerge from the tepee he shared with his uncle Mysterious Medicine. The man wore European clothing, but a closer look revealed him to be a Native American. Ohiyesa's first impulse was fear; his second was self-defence and he reached for his gun. Then he realized that his uncle, Mysterious Medicine, was walking confidently beside the newcomer. When Ohiyesa came face-to-face with the men, his uncle introduced his companion.

The young man learned with shock the identity of the stranger: he was Ohiyesa's father, Many Lightnings. To Ohiyesa, it seemed as if his father had returned from the spirit land, the eternal paradise of the dead. As the amazed young Sioux would soon learn, Many Lightnings's fate had been far different from the one his family believed he had met.

Many Lightnings had been one of the 264 men whose sentences President Lincoln had commuted, and he had

Ohiyesa's grandfather Seth Eastman was a brigadier general when this photograph was taken. Although Jacob Eastman had never met his wife's father, he adopted his name.

45

Residents chat outside their log cabin at Flandreau, the Santee reservation in South Dakota. Required to practice white customs if they remained at the settlement, the Sioux lived in houses instead of their traditional tepees.

spent three years in a federal prison in Davenport, Iowa. There, two missionaries, Dr. Thomas Williamson and Stephen Riggs, had taught Many Lightnings and some of his friends the ways of white culture. The missionaries had also converted them to Christianity. Many Lightnings, who had finally accepted the culture of his captors, had left the prison with a new name, Jacob Eastman.

After his release in 1866, Jacob Eastman had gone to live on the Santee reservation in Nebraska. But he and the heads of about 30 families found conditions on the reservation deeply dissatisfying, and they soon headed out, moving west and settling along South Dakota's Big Sioux River. Under the Homestead Act of 1862, they were legally entitled to the land if they used it as the government directed: instead of tepees, they were to build houses, and instead of hunting and gathering, they were to farm.

This experimental community, called Flandreau, became famous as one of the first government-sponsored Native American farming ventures. Here, said proud white officials, was an example of Indians who were willing and able to assimilate to white culture. The Great Mystery, Wankan Tanka, was no longer the center of their universe. Eastman and the Sioux families with whom he had founded the town now worshiped in the Presbyterian church. Jacob Eastman had concluded that it was useless to try to continue in the Sioux way. The Indian lifestyle was doomed to die; the whites had proven to be stronger. There was no choice but to forget the past, and to take on the white man's ways. The bravery Many Lightnings had demonstrated as a leader and a warrior was now expressed in his attitude toward his radically new lifestyle.

Jacob Eastman's arrival stirred much excitement in the Wahpeton camp. He spent several days telling his son and the other members of his old tiyospaye about his experiences and new ideas. Without question, he said, the Indian way of life had once been the best in the world. But there were also many virtues to white civilization. They had an involved system of measuring time—down to the last second. They knew how to write records of their history, and how to accumulate wealth for future generations. What was more, the whites had invented not only the guns, knives, hatchets, and pots that the Sioux had already incorporated into their own life but other amazing things as well.

Eastman had brought a pair of European-style trousers and a shirt for his son. He wanted to bring Ohiyesa back with him to Flandreau and send him to the white man's school. "It is true," Ohiyesa remembered his father saying, "that they have subdued and taught many peoples . . . but the sooner we accept their mode of life and follow their teaching, the better it will be for us all."

To Ohiyesa, Jacob Eastman must have seemed very strange. Not only had 10 years passed since Ohiyesa had last seen him, but now his father was an Indian in white man's clothes. His views contradicted everything Ohiyesa had been taught. But Ohiyesa listened respectfully to him. He did not question him, nor did he voice his doubts that

Ohiyesa's father, Many Lightnings, wears European clothing in a photograph from the early 1870s. By now known as Jacob Eastman, the Sioux patriarch had accepted Christianity and white culture, and he wanted Ohiyesa to do the same.

perhaps his father had given in to a false life. It was not for a Sioux to challenge his father, even if he had grown up without him.

But there was perhaps another reason why Ohiyesa gave careful consideration to his father's words. In his family, there had been others—his maternal great-grandfather, Cloud Man (Mahpiya Wichasta), born in 1783, for one—who had come to peaceful terms with the white men. Cloud Man had once been caught in a terrible blizzard. While lying buried in a snow bank, he had prayed to the Christian God, and vowed that if he survived he would follow the white man's ways.

True to his word, he later accepted Christianity, renounced hunting, and became a farmer. Moreover, he went on to establish a Sioux farming community in Eatonville, Minnesota. Throughout his life he was friendly to whites, often helping missionaries in their work among his people.

In 1830, not long after Cloud Man's conversion, Seth Eastman, a young captain of the United States Army, had come to Fort Snelling. Eastman had recently graduated from West Point, where, as a topographical engineer, he had distinguished himself for his remarkable drawing ability. Eastman was enthusiastic about Sioux culture. While stationed at Fort Snelling, he not only participated in buffalo hunts but spent much of his time drawing pictures of the Sioux in their traditional activities. He also became involved with a young Sioux woman, Stands Sacred, Cloud Man's daughter.

A year later, Stands Sacred gave birth to a little girl, Mary Nancy. It was she who later became so celebrated for her unusual beauty and intelligence that she was given the Sioux name Wakantankwanwin, or Goddess. Wakantankwanwin was Ohiyesa's mother.

That Ohiyesa's maternal grandfather was white may have contributed to the young man's willingness to try the white man's ways. The Sioux never forgot their ancestors, who, they believed, had power over the destiny of the living. Interestingly, when Many Lightnings had decided to change his name he chose the name of his dead wife's father. The memory of Seth Eastman had lingered, even in the consciousness of a man who had never met him.

Seth Eastman had abandoned his Sioux consort and child when Mary Nancy was three years old. The War Department, by his own request, had reassigned him to Louisiana to conduct a railroad survey. Eastman did

return 11 years later, not to visit his family but to be Fort Snelling's commander, a position he would hold for seven years. It is unclear whether he reestablished contact with his Indian family during this period. By then, he had a white wife, Mary Henderson Eastman. The Eastmans later retired to Washington, D.C., far away from Sioux territory.

While Seth Eastman was only a shadowy figure in Ohiyesa's family history, Cloud Man was not. Ohiyesa had personally met his great-grandfather. Cloud Man had visited Many Lightnings's camp when Ohiyesa was not quite four years old. Ohiyesa would later remember this

A Sioux warrior returns to his encampment outside Fort Snelling, Minnesota. Seth Eastman painted this view of the fort years after abandoning Stands Sacred and their daughter, Charles Eastman's mother.

visit with great pride. In his account, his great-grandfather, a dignified elderly man with pure white hair, had come for the sole purpose of meeting him—just as Ohiyesa's own father was to do a decade later.

And so it was not only with reluctance that Ohiyesa prepared to say goodbye to the only life he had ever known; he was also curious to experience for himself this way of life which others of his family had so readily endorsed. What would ease this transition to a strange life with a strange man would be the fact that he was not going alone. Surprisingly enough, Uncheedah, the strict traditionalist, had agreed to go with them. Mysterious Medicine, however, would remain behind. Nothing could convince him that his brother was right.

It was a dangerous journey back to the United States. But what Ohiyesa would remember most about this journey was not the fear of Ojibwa attacks, but his father's habit of beginning each day by reading a passage from the Bible and singing a hymn. A devout Christian, Jacob Eastman spoke often about Jesus Christ, trying to convert his son just as he himself had been converted by the missionaries. Christ had changed his life, he said. Indeed, it was because of Jesus that he had chosen to find his son.

By the conclusion of the journey, Ohiyesa, who had worshiped the Great Mystery all his life, agreed to be baptized. His father gave him a new name, one that would suit an Indian in white man's territory. Ohiyesa was now Charles Alexander Eastman.

6

NEW WHITE FATHERS

For Charles Eastman the first days of school were terrifying. A 14-year-old boy who had spent his entire life in the wilderness, he was expected to turn into an American schoolboy overnight. Instead of hunting and fighting in the open air, he was sitting on a stiff wooden bench in a crowded classroom, learning something called the ABCs. In his old life, he had felt himself a man, ready to prove himself on the warpath. Now he found himself unable to keep up with his 10-year-old classmates. He did not understand a word of English.

The other boys in the Flandreau mission school, all of them Sioux like himself, ridiculed this older new student who seemed so stupid. When one of them called him a baby, he stormed out of the classroom. As he jumped on his pony's back, the boys shouted insults after him, jeering at the "long-haired boy" and his "cowardice."

At last, Charles dismounted and took a walk in the woods—the only place where he felt at ease in this new country. After walking for some time, he reached a decision. He would go back to Canada to live with his uncle. Why suffer in a classroom to learn the ways of a people he did not understand and whom he had been trained to hate? The footprints of a bird were far more important to him than the incomprehensible letters that his teacher scribbled on the chalkboard.

That evening, Uncheedah saw that her grandson was upset and grew angry herself. A white education was an outrage for a Sioux, she said, and Charles was right to rebel. How could Jacob force his son to renounce everything he had grown up believing? Jacob Eastman responded firmly. There was no going back, he said. There was only one way for an Indian to advance, and that was through education. Did Charles want to be a "hobbled pony"? If he did not learn how to live among the whites, he was destined to be exactly that—a failed man without a future.

Charles Eastman never described his emotions as he stared at the fire while his father and grandmother argued that night. Whatever he felt, the next morning he had his long hair cut short and went back to school. But he was still far from sure that this path was the one for him. By accepting a white man's education, was he, as his grandmother said, betraying his people? Or was his father right when he said that the Sioux tradition could be welded to the white man's ways? According to his father, pursuing an education was similar to a hunter striving for success. Both required a sense of mission and the spirit of competition, and both resulted in a position of status.

After two years at the Flandreau school, Charles had decided on his course of action. He would, as he later wrote, "follow the new trail to the end." That fall, he would continue his education by enrolling in the Santee Normal School, an institution that trained teachers.

Students play football at the Flandreau mission school. Most Indian boys at the institution gave up lacrosse and other Sioux games in favor of "American" sports.

Wearing his hunting suit and carrying nothing but a blanket, an extra shirt and a gun, Charles set off for his new venture. He had a long journey before him: the school was on the Santee Indian reservation in Nebraska, more than 150 miles away. Charles and a neighbor, also on his way to the Santee reservation, would be making the journey together.

It was an adventure to travel across the wide prairies. "The whole country," as Eastman would later remember, "was practically uninhabited." For miles around, the travelers could see nothing but flowing grass and scattered patches of trees. Ducks flew in a cloudless blue sky and deer drank from ponds left by rainwater. Charles and his companion fed themselves by hunting these animals and trapping mink, otter, and

beaver. Every night they had a feast, roasting the game over a fire.

But on the third morning of the trip, Charles's fellow traveler said he had changed his mind. Why should he go live on a reservation when he could hunt and trap on the prairie, enjoying the freest life in the world? Charles, determined in his new course of action, would continue the trip by himself.

Traveling alone presented no problem to Charles, who was used to it. Still, it was with a certain amount of anxiety that he continued his journey. This would be the first time he would face white civilization by himself.

Sioux boys clean up the shop after a woodworking class at Flandreau. The mission school specialized in teaching Indian boys and girls the skills and crafts they would need as self-supporting members of white society.

Before, he always had his father or his companions at school to help him deal with whites. Two years in Flandreau had not been enough to make him feel comfortable with this strange people. In his mind, they were still the conquerors, a cold and distant race not to be trusted. And although he had learned to read and write English, he could not understand the Americans when they spoke to him.

But it was one experience with a white man during his trip that Charles would always remember. He had been walking all day, and was, as he later recalled, "hungry and thirsty as a moose." Eventually he came across a small sod farmhouse alongside a stream. A huge white man stood at the door, a shotgun in his hand. He looked gruff and unkempt, and a beard and mustache covered most of his face. Charles was too hungry to turn away. Looking directly at the man, he motioned that he wanted to buy food. His father had given him some money for the journey.

Without a word, the unsmiling farmer led Charles into the house where he introduced his grown son and four daughters. They stared silently at the young man, seemingly as afraid of him as he was of their father. The farmer waved him to the table, and he joined the others at dinner. To Charles, who sat on a rickety stool between the giant of a man and one of his daughters, everyone seemed uncomfortable. Suddenly the farmer struck the table with the butt of his knife, making the dishes shake. Charles jumped up, ready to defend himself. Then he glanced around the table, realized that this was the way the man signaled his family that he was about to say grace, and sat down quietly.

After dinner, Charles held out a handful of money, but the man shook his head. Finally smiling, he invited Charles to spend the night. Charles declined politely, knowing he would feel more comfortable outdoors. He had never slept in a white man's house. As Charles lay outside, he heard the sounds of music and laughter from the sod house. Overwhelmed by new impressions, he slept restlessly. For the first time whites did not seem like a hateful people.

Three days later, Charles arrived at the Santee Normal School, where he was welcomed by his brother John. John Eastman had stayed with their father after the Sioux Uprising, taken up the white man's ways, and was now an assistant teacher at the school. He would look after his little brother and make sure that he adjusted well to the new school.

The Santee Normal School had been founded in 1870 by Stephen R. Riggs, the Presbyterian minister who had taught Eastman's father. The idea of the school was to train Sioux to become what white society considered useful, responsible citizens who would return to influence their people with what they had learned. Students studied mathematics, music, reading, and writing, and were required to go to church and Sunday school.

Charles found it difficult to adjust to his new environment. Shy and intimidated by his teachers, he chose to spend most of his time alone, studying. This manner of coping served him well. After two years, his English had greatly improved and he had learned to read his own language. He had also become familiar with elementary algebra and geometry, particularly hard subjects for a boy who had grown up in a world that had no concept of—or need for—mathematics. He later recalled that at this point he still found something absurd in the concept that "everything must be measured in time or money or distance."

Alfred Riggs, the son of the school's founder, served as its superintendent. He soon took an interest in Charles,

John Eastman (seen in a 1904 photograph) was Charles's older brother. An assistant teacher at the Santee Normal School, he helped Charles adjust to life at the new institution.

whom he saw as the possessor of unusual energy and a determination to persevere in whatever task was set before him. Perhaps because of Riggs's encouragement, Charles soon decided that he wanted to go beyond the system of "Indian schools," which taught only basic skills. He began to dream of one day studying with white people in one of their schools. Supportive of the gifted young man's dream, Riggs saw to it that Charles received a scholarship to a two-year high school program at Beloit College in Wisconsin.

The night before he was to leave for college, Charles got shocking news from Flandreau: his father had died suddenly. Charles was now alone in an alien world; this time, he was sure, no father would come back from the spirit world to guide him. Feelings of anguish overwhelmed him. But the next morning, thinking of what his father would have wanted him to do, Charles Eastman boarded the train for Beloit.

As the train passed through the towns of the Midwest, Eastman was astounded by the wonders of "civilization": paved streets, horsedrawn buggies, stores, houses, bridges, restaurants. "Every hour brought new discoveries and new thoughts," he wrote, "visions that came and passed like the telegraphs we sped by."

Eastman's experience at Beloit was not a happy one. The year was 1876, and the United States had just suffered an infamous defeat at the hands of Sioux leaders Sitting Bull and Crazy Horse, who had annihilated the forces commanded by General George Armstrong Custer at the Battle of the Little Bighorn in Dakota Territory. At this point, many whites felt deep hostility toward Native Americans, especially Sioux—whose number, of course, included Charles Eastman. His classmates taunted him cruelly, calling him "Sitting Bull's nephew" and asking him if he planned to scalp them. When he went into town, other students bellowed war-whoops as he passed. To make it through each day of school, Eastman needed all the strength Mysterious Medicine had given him.

After three unhappy years at Beloit, Eastman followed Riggs's advice and enrolled at Knox College in Illinois, a school that would prepare him for college. In the memoirs that he wrote in later life, Eastman proudly noted that at Knox he became friends with students who would later become successful businessmen and lawyers. His pride in these friends may be revealing: in his eyes, the values of the "civilized" world had become highly important, and it was at this time that he decided to become a doctor.

In January 1882, Eastman traveled across the country to New England. Again on Riggs's suggestion, he had chosen Dartmouth College, a prestigious New Hampshire institution, as the place to pursue his studies. He now aimed to prove his ability among the nation's top students. The journey east proved to be another eye-opening experience. Where once the Illinois Indians had lived on the grassy shores of Lake Michigan now stood Chicago, a huge, bustling city of towering brick and stone. As the train continued eastward, the young scholar felt increasingly overwhelmed by the degree to which whites had taken over Native American territory. In New England, the white man's civilization was so firmly entrenched that it almost seemed to Eastman that no one else had ever lived there. "The day of the Indian," he mused sadly, "had passed forever."

For some time, Eastman had believed that his people might be better off if they tried to assimilate themselves into the new white civilization. Now he was absolutely convinced. He did not want the Sioux to disappear as had some eastern Native American tribes. As the train rolled past farmhouses and villages, he came to a conclusion he would support for the rest of his life: as he put it, "the Sioux should accept civilization before it was too late." This did not mean that he believed—or would ever believe—that European culture was superior to that of the Native Americans. It meant survival. He told himself that he would dedicate himself to helping his people achieve this goal.

The train's last stop was Boston, a city characterized by Eastman as oppressively filled with "old, mossy, granite edifices and narrow, crooked streets." Bostonians, he thought, were cold, unfriendly people who hurried along their business "as if a wolf was chasing them." To a man raised in the Sioux culture, where no one rushed through life or thought of time as "money," such hustling and bustling seemed unnatural.

In the fall of 1883, the 25-year-old Eastman enrolled as a freshman at Dartmouth. His experience at this highly regarded college was perhaps the most rewarding of his adult life so far. His classmates, most of them members of the well-to-do eastern establishment, were enthusiastic about their Indian peer. They invited him to join them in the card game whist, welcomed him into the fraternity life, and even elected him captain of the football team. A combination of curiosity about the "exotic Indian" and genuine respect for Eastman made him one of the most popular figures on campus.

During his four years at Dartmouth, Eastman pursued a rigorous academic program. He studied a wide variety of subjects—French, Latin, Greek, German, and English, as well as botany, zoology, chemistry, physics, natural history, philosophy, geometry, political science, and history—some of which he had never heard of

Eastman (top left) joins a group of fellow athletes at Dartmouth College. The strength and self-discipline he had developed as a young man enabled him to excel in all sports, from boxing to baseball to tennis.

10 years earlier. But Mysterious Medicine had trained his nephew well. Eastman, with his exceptional memory and powers of observation, managed to excel in almost every area.

Eastman was a good student, but he did not spend all his time studying. He spent three hours a day working out in a gym, a practice he would continue for many years after college. He also boxed, played football, baseball, and tennis, and starred on the track team, breaking the college's record for long-distance running. His Sioux upbringing had taught him to value the life of the body as much as the life of the mind.

Eastman was no longer the frightened, humiliated boy who ran out of the classroom at Flandreau. Tall, with strong features and the build of an athlete, Eastman had a commanding presence. He seemed at ease with everyone, even the students who had grown up in the wealthiest surroundings, and when he spoke, people listened. Pictures of the Dartmouth class of 1887 reveal Eastman's impact on his classmates: in each photograph, he sits at front row center. He had come a long way since his first school days—and this was only the beginning.

Among the friends Eastman made during his four years at Dartmouth were Frank Wood and his wife, Christian reformers who were sincerely interested in the contemporary movement to help Native Americans. The Woods had met Eastman when he first arrived in Boston and had subsequently made him a part of their family; Eastman, in fact, referred to them as a second mother and father. They introduced him to their friends, invited him along on their outings, and advised him about his dress and manners. They even helped him support himself by arranging for him to give lectures at Wellesley College.

But most of all, the Woods influenced the direction of Eastman's future. With other members of their activist circle, they raised money for him to go to Boston University Medical School, from which he graduated in 1890, a full-fledged doctor of medicine. Eastman's education—encouraged so generously by white benefactors—had persuaded him to think well of the civilization that had vanquished his own.

But Eastman would soon have a rude awakening.

7

DR. CHARLES
ALEXANDER EASTMAN

A few months after he graduated from medical school, Eastman learned that the government's Indian Service Bureau had rejected his request to serve as physician on a Sioux reservation. Instead, the bureau had appointed him to work among the Gros Ventres Indians of North Dakota. It was a strange choice. Not only were the Gros Ventres traditional enemies of the Sioux, but Eastman did not even know their language.

Understandably, the young physician was bitterly disappointed. What kind of doctor could he be, he asked himself, if he could not communicate with his patients? He wrote to the Indian Bureau, pleading for a change in assignment. "The government physician," he wrote, "can be the most useful civilizer among the force of government officers placed in any Indian Reservation if he could understand the language and the habits of the people."

After several insistent letters from Eastman as well as from his friend Frank Wood, the Indian Bureau agreed

A school building on the Pine Ridge reservation looms behind a Cheyenne woman and her child. The aim of such schools was to encourage Native American children to abandon their culture and assimilate into American society.

to change his assignment. But there was still a problem. The white physicians who were already at Sioux reservations did not want to give up their jobs for Eastman. Eventually, however, the bureau found him a place at the Pine Ridge Agency in South Dakota.

It was a dreary day when Eastman arrived at Pine Ridge. The reservation, consisting of a few houses scattered on the flat, dusty plains, seemed bleak and desolate. The mood of the Sioux who lived there was similar to that of their landscape. Their crops had failed that year, and the U.S. government had cut their food rations. To add to their woes, they had been battling epidemics of cholera and other diseases brought back to them from Sioux who had gone to Europe as members of the "Wild West" shows then popular both in the United States and abroad.

Eastman moved into his quarters, a bare wooden building furnished only with a few hard wooden chairs, and set up his office. He immediately recognized the vast scope of his new job: to start with, he was the only doctor on the reservation, responsible for the health of more than 6,000 people. Sanitary conditions were primitive, and the reservation seethed with disease, which spread from one cabin to the next, quickly contaminating whole settlements.

Eastman, however, found no time to brood about the difficulties of his new job. From almost the moment of his arrival at the reservation, he worked around the clock, treating his patients both in his office and at their homes. He often traveled many miles on horseback to visit those who were bedridden, and he regularly came close to falling asleep on his horse. Eastman's approach, he learned, was nothing like that of his predecessor, a bored and resentful white doctor who had merely filled prescriptions without bothering even to examine his patients.

Then something happened that made reservation life quite different for the doctor. On one of his rare free afternoons, he accepted an invitation to a tea party held by the white staff members of the reservation's schools. Like other generous-spirited humanitarians of the day, many of these teachers felt a collective guilt about the nation's treatment of Native Americans, and they wanted to do their share in helping to make amends. Strange as the idea may seem in the late 20th century, these idealists believed the only way to help the Indians was to assist them in shedding their own culture and adopting that of mainstream America.

Sioux who refused to move onto reservations continued to live in camps such as this one, photographed near Pine Ridge in 1891.

At the party, one of these teachers caught Eastman's eye. She was, he discovered, Elaine Goodale, an idealistic Massachusetts teacher who had come west to help the Sioux assimilate. Twenty-seven years old when she met Eastman, Goodale had already been promoted to the position of government supervisor of the Sioux schools in the Dakotas and Nebraska. Eastman and Goodale found that they had a lot in common. Both were dedicated to the cause of Native American improvement, and both believed that the path lay through education.

Goodale, as she revealed in her later memoirs, was struck by Eastman's energy and charm. She was also happy that he seemed to find her attractive, particularly as she believed that most people considered her cold and distant. Perhaps, she thought, her bold ways alienated people. Ever since she was a child, she had distinguished herself for her sharp mind and talent for writing. At the age of 15, she and her sister Dora published *Apple Blossoms*, a book of sentimental poetry that had become a national best-seller.

Eastman had met many impressive New England women when he was at Dartmouth, but Goodale seemed extraordinary to him. Here was someone who embraced, as he did, two cultures. Goodale came from an old New England family, as had Eastman's grandfather Seth Eastman. At the age of 20, she decided to work as a missionary teacher to Native Americans in the Berkshire Hills of western Massachusetts. After that, she took a job at Virginia's Hampton Institute, which was founded to bring up Indian boys in the style of white Americans.

After a year of teaching and writing press releases for the Institute, Goodale decided to go west and work directly with the Sioux. She knew it would mean a lonely lifestyle, far from family and friends, but the move would also guarantee a kind of freedom that 19th-century

Charles Eastman and Elaine Goodale appear in portraits taken in 1890. The two became engaged four days before the massacre at Wounded Knee.

women rarely experienced. At the Pine Ridge reservation, she had complete command of the schools. She was also able to go hiking and horseback riding in the woods by herself, and she had time to write. She wrote numerous essays and articles about her experiences, many of which were published in eastern newspapers.

One month after they met, Elaine Goodale and Charles Eastman announced their engagement to be married. Strongly attracted to each other and compatible in their interests, they were sure they were destined to be together. The fact that they were from different racial backgrounds seemed to strengthen their bond; each had always been fascinated with the culture of the other.

The courtship between Eastman and Goodale coincided with one of the most tense periods in the history of Native American–white relations. Ghost dancing, the new religious movement founded by the medicine man

Wovoka, had begun to spread. From one reservation to the next, it attracted a stream of new believers with its powerful message: that the time of oppression would soon be over. Ever since Eastman had arrived in November, government Indian agents had been peppering Washington, D.C., with requests for troops to suppress the movement. It was a "time of grim suspense," noted Goodale in her memoirs. "We seemed to be waiting," she added, "helplessly waiting—as if in some horrid nightmare, for the inevitable catastrophe."

Eastman urged his superiors at the agency to be patient. It would be better to try to reason with the leaders of the Ghost Dance, he argued, than to risk violence by confronting them with military might. And what power did the defeated Native Americans have, now that they were reduced to reporting to the agency and living on government subsidies? Furthermore, asserted Eastman, not a single Ghost Dance leader advocated violence. They expected their hopes to be fulfilled by supernatural forces that would cause the whites to disappear miraculously. Their land would be magically rejuvenated, with new grass covering the continent and millions of buffalo returning to roam the prairies. It was a vision of paradise—the last illusion of a desperate people.

Four days after Goodale and Eastman announced their engagement, the slaughter at Wounded Knee took place. Working at agency headquarters at the time, Eastman first heard the distant thunder of a cannon, then nearby hoofbeats of a galloping horse. Seconds later, a messenger rode furiously up with a grim report: the Seventh Cavalry had fired on Big Foot's band and killed hundreds of people. Panicked, the Pine Ridge whites started dismantling their tents and preparing to flee. In the interim, they placed sentinels with machine guns at strategic points around the reservation.

The Pine Ridge Indian police line up for dress inspection around 1880. Eastman managed to stop the shooting that erupted between the Sioux and the Indian police following the Battle of Wounded Knee.

Equally alarmed, the reservation Sioux began shooting at the sentinels, wounding two of them. Others started to burn buildings. The Indian police—Sioux who worked for the federal government—were firing on the milling crowd when Eastman stepped in and ordered them to stop shooting. Then he shouted at the angry Sioux and told them it was useless to continue. The gunfire soon ceased, but the relationship between the Indians and whites remained tense.

The wounded and the dead were brought into the chapel. Many, Eastman remembered, "were frightfully torn by pieces of shells." But Eastman did not see the full extent of the carnage until three days later, when he and a party of soldiers trekked through the snow to Wounded Knee. There, among the fragments of burned tepees, frozen bodies lay in the snow, some piled on top of each other. A few Indians had managed to crawl away to a log shed nearby, but most of these had died in the cold. Bodies were scattered along the road and in the woods, their limbs protruding from the snowdrifts. East-man did manage to find a few survivors, an elderly woman lying unconscious under a wagon and an infant girl protected from the snow by her mother's dead body. The child was wearing a hat embroidered with the American flag.

"All this was a severe ordeal for one who had so lately put all his faith in the Christian love and lofty ideals of the white man," Eastman wrote in his autobiography. Only two months before, he had been in Boston, enjoying the conversation of Christian reformer friends who fervently believed in Native American assimilation projects. Indeed, that summer he had spoken in favor of the 1887 Dawes General Allotment Act, the law that was principally responsible for the desperate conditions among the Sioux.

Eastman had thought that the Dawes Act, which divided the reservations into individual lots, would empower the Indians. By learning how to farm and manage property, he believed, they could grasp the values of the white man, just as he had through his schooling. What Eastman did not know was that through the Dawes Act the Indians would lose over 80 million acres of land—two-thirds of what they owned. The law specified that all "surplus" land not distributed in allotments was open for sale to whites. Eastman had been persuaded to believe that the white men were looking out for the good of his people. Wounded Knee told a different story.

The victims of Wounded Knee were buried in a mass grave. (The U.S. government later ordered their bodies exhumed for scientific studies.) The children who

Soldiers help bury the Wounded Knee Indian dead in a mass grave. Recalling the grim scene, a civilian gravedigger said, "It was a thing to melt the heart of a man, if it was of stone, to see those little children, with their bodies shot to pieces, thrown naked into the pit."

survived were placed with white families. Eastman noted without irony the kindness of these families, who would bring up the Sioux orphans as Christians. Yet other comments he made show that his faith in Christianity, as practiced by whites, was sorely tested by the events of 1890. "Many Indians now believe in Christ's teachings as explained to them by their missionaries," he wrote in an impassioned article, "but they find it impossible to believe that this Government is Christian, or the average official an honest man."

Eastman's disappointment with white government leaders did not extend to his feelings for Elaine Goodale. The two were married six months later in a church wedding in New York City. Newspapers made much of what was perceived to be a scandalous union. An interracial marriage was, in 1891, an affront to the sensibility of many white Americans. Later, Goodale would feel compelled to explain in her memoirs why she "had made a gift of herself" to a Sioux.

The wedding was followed by a lavish reception hosted by the Woods. Many Christian reformers and other members of the New England elite came to toast the new couple. It was a far cry from the type of marriage celebration that Eastman's ancestors had experienced. In the Sioux culture, a marriage is a private affair. The couple quietly sets up a home together, publicly acknowledging the union months later.

Eastman's own parents, Many Lightnings and Wakantankwanwin, had eloped. Wakantankwanwin had waited for the man she was in love with to come, with a blanket over his head, to take her from her family's tepee. The man she expected, however, was not Many Lightnings, but another young warrior. Many Lightnings had heard about the plan, and, in love with Wakantankwanwin himself, came in the other man's stead, his identity disguised by the blanket. When Wakantankwanwin learned of the deception, she nevertheless agreed to stay with Many Lightnings. It was her belief that Wankan Tanka had punished her for disobeying her father, and that she should accept her fate.

The difference between Eastman's courtship and his father's shows how far Eastman had grown from his

Sioux culture. Despite Wounded Knee, he was still dedicated to the cause of assimilation. In the summer of 1891, he and Goodale returned to Pine Ridge, where they planned to continue their work among the Sioux. They had no way of knowing what trouble was in store for them.

8

EASTMAN VERSUS BROWN

Eastman cuddles his first child, Dora. As he tried to expose bureaucratic corruption, the young doctor's life at Pine Ridge became increasingly difficult, but Dora's arrival helped ease the tensions.

Something suspicious was happening at the Pine Ridge Agency. The U.S. government had recently sent the $100,000 it had promised to those Sioux who had been "nonhostile" during the Ghost Dance troubles. This was to be their recompense for the property and cattle they lost as a result of the military crackdown. Many Sioux, however, after receiving their allotment from the agency office, suspected that they had not been given their full share.

Could it be, the Sioux asked themselves, that James Cooper, the special agent in charge of disbursement, was taking advantage of the fact that few of them knew how to count? What made this seem likely was that those who did understand the white man's numbers were not permitted to remain at the desk and count the money. Each Sioux had been hastily given his share, then told to make room for the next. Many of the Sioux later claimed to have discovered that the money was 10 to 20 percent less than it should have been.

The Sioux chose to take their problem to Eastman, the highest-ranking Indian on the reservation, and one with connections not only to Cooper but to officials in Washington, D.C. The complaints were serious. The Sioux claimed that Cooper, secretly in league with other whites on the reservation, was actually involved in many schemes to defraud the Indians of their land and money. Corruption, they claimed, was endemic in the Indian agency. Eastman immediately set about writing letters to his friends in Washington. He had learned how effective newspaper articles and essays had been in raising the national consciousness about the horror of Wounded Knee. Perhaps a written account of the corruption at Pine Ridge would be enough to prod the government into cleaning up the situation.

The official in charge of the Wounded Knee Agency was Captain George Le Roy Brown. When he heard that Eastman was complaining about his operation to people outside the reservation, he became furious. To him, it was an outrage that this new doctor had dared to go behind his back to defend the Indians. Because Eastman worked for the government, Brown held that his first loyalty should be to the United States and the agency, not to his people.

Brown wrote the commissioner of Indian Affairs in Washington, giving his version of the story. He also made a scathing commentary on Eastman's rash behavior. The doctor, he wrote, had taken a few men's words as the truth, and then, without investigating the validity of the charges, had taken it upon himself to slander the reservation. Brown's men were innocent, he said. In fact, Cooper himself had ordered an investigation of the charges and had found that they had no basis.

Shawled against the biting North Dakota winter, Sioux women wait for rations at Pine Ridge in 1891. Most of the reservation's residents believed that Indian agents were cheating them out of the recompense promised by the U.S. government.

Eastman wrote his own letter to Commissioner Thomas Morgan, explaining why he had taken his position. What followed was an epistolary war. For the next year, Brown and Eastman continued to send the commissioner letters, each arguing his own side of the matter. Eventually, the men no longer disguised their hatred of each other, each openly assaulting the other's character. Eastman wrote Morgan that Brown's honesty was questionable; once, he said, Brown had tried to get him involved in a scheme in which he was to buy Sioux cattle at a low price and then sell it to whites at a higher price.

Eastman also said that Brown had treated him as an inferior, acting in a way that suggested that an Indian doctor was not worthy of respect. He would send Eastman to patients miles away on the reservation, and then, after Eastman was well into the journey, would have a messenger ride out and order him to return at once. Eastman would then have exhausted his horses for nothing.

Brown maintained that it was Eastman, not himself, who had the dubious moral character. The doctor, he asserted, had tried to persuade him to get the Sioux to sell their land. Trying to bolster his complaints about Eastman, Brown said he lacked respect for government property, even riding his horses to the point of exhaustion.

In September 1892, more than a year after the original incident, Brown formally requested that Eastman be transferred out of the agency. Morgan responded by sending Eastman several offers for positions at other agencies, including the one at Flandreau where Eastman had gone to school. Eastman refused them all. "I have now fully decided," he wrote, "to stand my ground—not for a personal advantage or any desire of my own benefit . . . but for the sake of principle and self-respect."

Tending to believe Eastman, the commissioner said Brown was acting like "a petty tyrant." Other influential whites also supported Eastman: his loyal friend, Frank Wood, and Senator Henry Dawes, author of the Dawes Act, both wrote letters on his behalf. But perhaps Eastman's strongest ally was his wife, who wrote numerous newspaper articles criticizing the conditions at the Pine Ridge reservation and Brown's management of it. Newspapers across the country published her reports.

Goodale's articles infuriated Brown, who mobilized his own supporters to write to the newspapers in his defense. The war of letters escalated into a national contest of power. On January 5, 1893, President Benjamin Harrison directed Eastman to come to meet Secretary of the Interior John Noble in Washington, D.C., "upon business that would be made known to him on his arrival."

In the meantime, Noble sent investigators to check the validity of the Indians' claims. One investigation found that Cooper had, as claimed, shortchanged the Indians. Dissatisfied with the report, Noble ordered another

The 2nd Infantry camps on the Pine Ridge reservation. Eastman's assertions of corruption by Indian agents angered Captain George Le Roy Brown, who succeeded in having the doctor removed from his post at the reservation.

investigation. This one found Cooper completely innocent and repudiated the earlier findings. The Sioux, the report said, had not been cheated out of a penny.

Despite the findings of the investigation, Brown worried that Eastman would use his visit to Washington to bring the government officials over to his side. He wrote to officials in the capital, asking for the opportunity to plead his own case, but he received no response.

When Eastman returned to Pine Ridge, he found a surprise awaiting him. Brown had locked the doors to his office and retracted his right to practice medicine on the reservation. If Washington refused to get rid of Eastman, he would do it himself. He followed his drastic action by writing a letter to Herbert Welsh, secretary of the Indian Rights Association, accusing Eastman of continuing to treat him disrespectfully. At that point, Eastman had been back exactly one day.

Neither Brown nor Eastman would budge and the situation became intolerable. In the long run, however, it was Brown who ran the reservation. On January 25, 1893, Secretary Noble suspended Eastman from his duties at Pine Ridge and ordered his transfer to another agency. All the evidence pointed, he said, to Brown's impeccable character. And although he could find nothing wrong with Eastman, the doctor would have to go in order for Brown to maintain his authority on the reservation.

Eastman preferred to resign. In February 1893, along with his wife and newborn daughter, Dora, he left Pine Ridge reservation and went to St. Paul, Minnesota. The dream of working for his people had proved a failure. Now Eastman would settle down and set up a medical practice to support his growing family. It would be a quiet existence, a relief after the stress and anguish of the previous two years. But as things turned out, Dr. Charles Eastman would not remain quiet for long.

9

▼ ▽ ▼

BETWEEN TWO WORLDS

To afford the move to St. Paul, the Eastmans had been forced to sell their furniture, and now they were trying to make ends meet by taking in boarders. The couple was running out of money. Not many white people visited Native American physicians, and those who did expected exotic Indian cures and medicines. Eastman, however, flatly refused, as one businessman suggested he do, to exploit his Sioux heritage and pretend to be a medicine man.

Eastman's patients slowly began to increase in number, but he discovered that a private practice was not for him. He had higher aims, and struggling to pursue an ordinary medical career made him restless. He wanted to use his strengths and talents to help his people. In the winter of 1893, he wrote to the Indian service and asked for reinstatement. The service replied that it had no openings. Then another organization, the Young Men's Christian Association (YMCA), offered him the position of secretary.

The Young Men's Christian Association (YMCA) established this outpost on the Pine Ridge reservation to teach Christian values to the Sioux. Eastman worked for the YMCA so that he could help other Native Americans adjust to white society.

85

The YMCA was an organization founded in 1844 to teach people, through social activities, to be upright Christian citizens. The association had experienced recent success with its Indian programs and wanted to expand them throughout the country. As YMCA secretary, Eastman would be responsible for investigating existing programs and starting up new ones. To Eastman, this job seemed perfect. He was to help others adjust to white civilization and Christian beliefs, just as he himself had done. As a Sioux who had taken the same path, he could contribute an unusual perspective and would be better able to understand the deficiencies of the schools.

To investigate YMCA programs at Indian schools and reservations, Eastman traveled to Pennsylvania, Kansas, North and South Dakota, and Nebraska. He often met with groups of young men—Sioux, Cheyenne, Cree, and even Ojibwa, his old enemy—to teach them about Christianity. Not surprisingly, his greatest success was among his own people, the Sioux.

At the end of one year, Eastman had strong recommendations for the improvement of the programs. The YMCA, he said, should train more Indians to be leaders and should set up summer camps for this purpose. It should also reinforce the connections between YMCAs on reservations and those at Indian schools. The YMCA put Eastman's suggestions into practice with successful results.

Eastman's relationship to his work was not without its conflicts. There he was, spreading Christianity for the YMCA, even though he doubted the sincerity of many white Christians. "They spoke much of spiritual things," he wrote, "while seeking only the material." He could not help but agree with the protests he heard from the Indians to whom he preached. One elderly warrior, after a week of Bible study with Eastman, announced that he was sure Jesus Christ was an Indian. No white man he knew, said the warrior, followed the principles of peace and brotherly love that were commonly observed by his people.

Eastman shared this view. "I confess I have wondered much that Christianity is not practiced by the very people who vouch for that wonderful conception of exemplary living," he wrote. "It appears that they are anxious to pass on their religion to all races of men, but keep very little of it themselves."

Eastman was also aware of the spirit of conquest that pervaded Christian missionary work. In his book *The Soul of the Indian*, he tells the story of a missionary who tried to teach the Indians the biblical account of creation. The Indians listened courteously to the tale of Adam and Eve, then returned the favor by telling the missionary a story of their own about the origin of maize. The missionary reacted with indignation. In disgust, he accused the Indians of continuing to believe in falsehoods. The Indians flinched at this rude response. "Here we believed your story," one of them said, "but now you refuse to believe ours." To Eastman, the story suggested that Indians, perhaps, were more genuinely "civilized" than their conquerors.

Eastman also felt that Native Americans were more profoundly religious than whites. Christians, he noted, set aside one day a week to worship, but Indians worshiped every day. They were never without a sense of wonder for the Great Mystery. Eastman offered the example of a hunter who would often pause in the course of his daily work to contemplate the beauty and power of nature. After killing an animal, he would smoke a pipe in a symbolic offering to Wankan Tanka. In the Sioux culture, explained Eastman, "Every act of life is, in a very real sense, a religious act."

Eastman, who saw the drawbacks of "civilization," continued to work in its service. He believed that the only way to advance in a technological society was to accept the culture of those who ran it. Moreover, he made a distinction between the spirit of Christianity and the way it was practiced, and was never dissuaded from his own belief in the virtues of Christian ideals. For him, the Christian message was similar to the one he was taught as a boy. Both the Sioux religion and Christianity emphasized self-sacrifice, disregard of material possessions, and generosity to the poor. Both believed in a great God whose spirit was manifested in nature. "The spirit of Christianity and of our ancient religion," Eastman concluded, "is essentially the same."

Eastman took great pains to draw similarities between Christianity and the Sioux religion. He compared the Christian sacrament of confirmation to the Sioux *bambeday* rite, in which a young boy fasted for two days alone in the woods in order to receive the spirit of Wankan Tanka. He mentioned that while Christians were in awe of the miraculous Virgin birth of Christ, Indians bowed before the miracle of all human births. Eastman may have made such comparisons because he wanted to convince himself that it was indeed possible to merge both cultures.

On one of his trips for the YMCA, Eastman met a Scottish missionary who said that he owed his Christian beliefs to a Sioux. As a young man, the Scot had spent his life traveling from place to place. One winter, while in Manitoba, Canada, he met a Sioux warrior who had recently converted to Christianity. This man spoke so eloquently about the Christian faith that the Scot was moved to convert. To Eastman's astonishment, he learned that the fervent Christian warrior was none

Students perform experiments in a physics laboratory at the Carlisle Indian School in 1915. When Eastman worked at the school in 1899, he drew on his experience as a Native American who had struggled with the process of assimilation.

other than his uncle, Mysterious Medicine, who had become a pious farmer.

Eastman arranged to have one of his missions take him to Canada so he could see his uncle. Little is known about the reunion between the men, both of whom had changed radically since they had last seen each other more than 20 years earlier. All that Eastman wrote about this meeting is that he was satisfied that his old teacher had taken the path that he had taken himself. While Eastman was in Canada he also paid his respects to his grandmother's grave. Uncheedah was dead, and so too was the kind of life she had led.

Eastman worked for the YMCA from 1895 to 1899. During that time, he became thoroughly committed to assimilation projects. In 1899—his assignment with the YMCA completed—he accepted a position at the Carlisle School in Pennsylvania, one of the most famous Indian institutions in the country. Founded in 1879, the Carlisle School aimed to teach Indian boys and girls such basic industrial skills as carpentry and metalwork. The children were placed in white families, as was the case with the Hampton Institute, where Elaine Goodale had taught. Colonel Richard Henry Pratt, Carlisle's superintendent, had designed the school to help Indians become like "young Anglo-Saxons." It was Eastman's job to check the students' progress in the families and recommend ways to help ease the tension of the bicultural experience.

Eastman was happy at the Carlisle School, but he and his wife now had four children, and he needed more than the $800 yearly salary offered by the school. Thus, when the Indian service offered him the position of agency physician of the Crow Creek reservation, he took it after serving only one year at Carlisle. Eastman looked forward to the chance to practice medicine for his people, as he had originally planned to do when he left college.

The Crow Creek salary was more than 50 percent higher than the Carlisle salary, but it was money earned dearly. Eastman's experience at Crow Creek repeated the events at Pine Ridge. Once again he found himself caught in the middle of a tense feud between the reservation Indians and the official in charge of the agency, Harry Chamberlain. The Indians suspected Chamberlain of running the reservation with an eye to his own profits and voiced their complaints to Eastman. They hoped that Eastman, who had a foot in both the white and the Sioux cultures, would help them. Chamberlain anticipated problems. He feared the kind of influence that the renowned doctor would have with Washington officials and soon requested that Eastman be transferred.

Chamberlain buttressed his request by accusing Eastman of everything from medical negligence to immoral behavior. Among other charges, he asserted that Eastman had examined a woman, Augusta Hultman, without a third person present, a violation of the era's strict rules of medical propriety. Hultman, superintendent of the Grace Boarding School, was suspended from her position—a verdict she later successfully challenged on grounds of discrimination. Eastman, on the other hand, was reprimanded but kept his position. Nevertheless, unpleasant rumors continued to fly. They were undoubtedly all circulated by Chamberlain in his attempts to discredit the doctor who threatened his own reputation.

The tension on the reservation reached a climax when a fight erupted involving Charles Eastman, Augusta Hultman, and Henrietta Freemont, the schoolteacher who had reported Eastman's alleged indiscretion to the authorities. Freemont began screaming at Hultman and Eastman, accusing them of bringing a bad name to the school and of humiliating her personally. The incident ended with Freemont striking Hultman in the face.

This fight was the last straw. Inspector Frank Churchill came from Washington to make a thorough investigation of the troubles at Crow Creek. He offered a drastic solution: to close the Crow Creek school and transfer all the teachers. Although he concluded that Eastman and Hultman were innocent, he punished them anyway. After filing a sharp criticism of Hultman, he recommended that her salary be cut. As for Eastman, he was to be transferred to another agency, one where he did not speak the language. Eastman, Churchill argued, was "a dangerous man to have on a reservation where the Dakota or Sioux language is spoken."

Churchill's comments betray the real reasons Eastman found himself in such difficulties at the Crow Creek reservation. Eastman's performance as a physician was, by many reports, exemplary. Health conditions had improved significantly in the three years he held his position. He had even prevented a smallpox epidemic. As for charges of marital infidelity, not one of them was ever substantiated.

It was evident that the real reason for Eastman's dismissal lay elsewhere. As a Sioux with contacts in Washington, who both spoke the language and understood the problems of his people, Eastman was, as Churchill put it, "dangerous." Like few others, he was in a position to challenge the agency's often unscrupulous practices.

Eastman was forced to resign on March 12, 1903. What made the defeat tolerable was that the commissioner of Indian Affairs, William Jones, had an interesting job waiting for Eastman. He was not to be a doctor, nor was he to work on a reservation. The position would require Eastman to do something quite challenging and new for him: name his people.

Under the Dawes Severalty Act of 1887, the Great Sioux reservation had been parceled out in "allotments" to individual Sioux. The distribution of the property, however, proved problematic. The Indians had no surnames. How was the United States's legal system to keep track of property ownership and adjudicate the claims of heirs? Indians' names told nothing about their relationship to other people in their family. Wives had different names from husbands; children had different names from parents. Moreover, Indians usually had more than one name during a lifetime. With such a naming system, the Indians would not easily be able

Young Man Afraid of His Horse stands before his tepee at Pine Ridge in 1891. When the U.S. government assigned Eastman to give the Sioux new names, he was instructed to replace those that might sound humorous in English.

to prove ownership, which meant that they could be swindled out of their land.

At stake were not only property rights but the full acceptance of Indians in white society. Indian names sounded strange, sometimes even humorous, to whites. Indians were usually named after animals, special events, personal characteristics, and extraordinary achievements. Many names, such as Skunk's father or Red Nose's Mother, sounded derogatory to non-Indian ears. To a Sioux called Young Man Afraid of His Horse, his name was not an embarrassment; but it became so when dealing with white Americans.

The U.S. government had long considered a program to give the Indians new names but little had been accomplished. Then, in 1903, Hamlin Garland, an author and enthusiastic defender of Indian rights, took it upon himself to rally support for the name project's implementation. Garland convinced President Theodore Roosevelt of the project's importance and was chosen to be its director. The next step was to find the right person to perform the job. Eastman was the man.

Eastman approached the project of renaming the Sioux with great sensitivity to the desires and cultural traditions of his people. Garland had given him three basic guidelines to follow: the names had to be easy to pronounce; Indian names that sounded degrading in English had to be eliminated; and, whenever possible, the new names were to be similar in sound or meaning to the Indian names. Eastman added his own guidelines. As he put it, "My method was to select from the personal names of a family, one which should be reasonably short, euphonious, and easily pronounced by the white man in the vernacular." He tried to make the new names sound as beautiful and meaningful to the Sioux as their own names had been. For example,

The five Eastman daughters assemble on the lawn outside their home in Amherst, Massachusetts. During the six years that Charles Eastman spent renaming the Sioux, he had little time for his family.

"Bob-tailed Coyote" became "Robert T. Wolf" and "Rotten Pumpkin" became "Robert Pumpian."

Some of the Sioux were suspicious of the renaming project, believing, wrote Eastman, that this was just "another scheme of the white man to defraud them of the little land still left in their possession." But for the most part, the Sioux were willing to comply. Eastman gained their trust by his tireless commitment to the demanding job. He not only had to pick names for each individual person, he also had to conduct interviews and do extensive research to make sure all members of a family were grouped under one name. This was often difficult because of factors such as separation, remarriages, illegitimate children, and the Sioux custom of polygamy.

The project took six years, from 1903 until 1909. During that time, Eastman traveled to every Sioux reservation in the country. He rarely had a chance to visit with his family, which during this period had taken up residence in Amherst, Massachusetts, close to Elaine Eastman's childhood home. The Eastmans now had five daughters—Dora, Irene, Virginia, Eleanor, and Florence—and one son, Ohiyesa II. While Eastman advanced in his career, his wife stayed home and raised the children. This was later to be a contentious issue between them.

By 1909, Eastman had named the entire Sioux Nation—more than 25,000 people. It was one of his greatest achievements. Soon afterward, reports showed a reduction in property conflicts and land speculation. The Sioux, in appreciation of Eastman's work, gave him a name: the Name-Giver.

No one else was ever to accomplish what Eastman had done singlehandedly. Other tribes proved more difficult to rename, perhaps because those responsible lacked Eastman's sensitivity and commitment. Whatever the reason, the U.S. government eventually lost interest in naming the other tribes, and the project was scrapped after Eastman's success with the Sioux.

Charles Eastman, the Name-Giver, never fully gave up his own Indian name. Throughout his life, he used Ohiyesa and Charles Eastman interchangeably, signing all documents and letters with both names. Perhaps by this symbolic gesture he meant to show that he continued to be a Sioux, despite his acculturation in white society. It also reflected his commitment to an almost impossible mission: making Ohiyesa and Charles Alexander Eastman one person.

10

▼ ▼ ▼

TO HIS PEOPLE'S DEFENSE

While Charles Eastman was working as a doctor in St. Paul, he had begun writing the memoirs of his Sioux upbringing, anxious to preserve in print a way of life that no other generation would ever experience. Elaine Goodale, a writer herself, encouraged her husband in his project, eventually persuading him to submit his sketches to a magazine for publication. She not only recognized Eastman's potential as a spokesman for his people but hoped that his writing, like her own, could bring in extra money for the household.

The Eastmans' efforts to publish met with immediate success. The editors of *St. Nicholas*, a magazine for young people, enjoyed Eastman's lively accounts of his education under Uncheedah and Mysterious Medicine, and published them in a series of six articles. In 1902, Eastman compiled the articles into a book, *Indian Boyhood*, which became an immediate best-seller. In fact, the book met with such public favor that it was later published in a school edition.

Encouraged by the success of *Indian Boyhood*, Eastman went on to write and publish 10 other books as well as countless articles. Some of his writings, such as *Indian Boyhood* and its sequel *From the Deep Woods to Civilization*, published in 1916, were autobiographical. In other writings, Eastman presented and explained Indian culture to white readers. In doing so, he aimed to combat a prevailing notion that whites did not need to feel any guilt for having destroyed Indian culture because they thought themselves superior. Indian culture needed its defenders. Even many dedicated "Friends of the Indians" believed that Indian culture was a relic of the Stone Age and had nothing to offer the modern world.

In articles such as "The Indian's Gift to America," "Recollections of the Wild Life," and "Indian Handicrafts," Eastman impressed on his audience the virtues of the Indians' way of life, putting special emphasis on their harmonious coexistence with the natural world and the strong ethical codes that governed their everyday life. He also pointed out what the whites had learned from Indians: new methods of growing fruits and vegetables, as well as new ways to make medicines. Moreover, Americans, with their growing fondness for machine-made products, could well take a lesson, Eastman said, from the Indians, who made everything they owned by hand. Their intricately made handicrafts—such as pottery, jewelry, pipes, and beaded clothing—were a testimony to the beauty of the Indian world.

Eastman also wrote several books for children in which he retold the Indian legends he had heard as a boy. In the Sioux culture, people often spent their nights around a campfire telling stories. It was the children's responsibility to learn these stories by heart, so that they could one day relate them to the next generation. Storytelling was an important means for Indians to transmit their history and culture, serving as books did for literate peoples. Eastman, in telling these stories to a white audience, was continuing the tradition in the only way he felt he could. Instead of teaching Indian children, he would teach whites to understand a culture that was disappearing rapidly.

In all his works, Eastman never forgot that he was writing for a white audience. The virtues of his culture that he chose to discuss were those he believed white Americans would appreciate. For example, he emphasized Indians' religious piety, conscious that Indians would meet with more approval from Christian readers if they seemed devout. Similarly, he emphasized Indian women's chastity and commitment to motherhood, idealized qualities in the post–Victorian era. Like the idealized white woman of the day, the Indian woman, wrote Eastman, was "the silent but telling power behind life's activities." She quietly nurtured her husband and family and was a model of "feminine dignity and modesty." With statements such as these, Eastman hoped to prove that Indians were, as he put it, "a God-fearing, clean and honorable people before the coming of the white man."

Eastman had a practical motive for stressing the virtues of Indians that would appeal to whites. As well as wanting Indians to be accepted into American society, he wanted American citizenship for all Indians. At the time in which he wrote, Indians could only obtain citizenship if they met certain requirements, and even then they were not entirely trusted as equal citizens. Eastman made it his duty to persuade Americans that Indians could "contribute to the essential resources of the American nation."

For example, in *The Indian Today,* one of his most ambitious works in this direction, Eastman introduces "the Indian" to us as a model American citizen, as committed to the democratic ideal as the Founding

This photograph of Eastman appeared in From the Dark Woods to Civilization. *Although generally optimistic, the book revealed Eastman's misgivings about certain aspects of white civilization.*

Fathers: "In the first place, he is free born, hence a free thinker. His government is a pure democracy, based solidly upon intrinsic right and justice, which governs, in his conception, the play of life." In the same work, Eastman also remarks that American Indians had proven their commitment to the United States during World War I, when 10,000 Indians, among them Eastman's son, Ohiyesa II, served in the U.S. military.

Eastman's eagerness to please his white audiences, however, was often matched by a contradictory urge to rant against them. At the same time that his writing lauds the United States and tries to show how the Indian will contribute to the country, Eastman makes critical comments about the virtues of the Indians' conquerors. Even in such seemingly optimistic works as *From the Dark Woods to Civilization,* he often betrays a sense of disillusionment and anger with the "so-called civilization" to which his father had introduced him. "When I reduce civilization to its lowest terms," he wrote, "it becomes a system of life based upon trade. The dollar is the measure of value, and might still spells right; otherwise, why war?"

Eastman was particularly disgusted by the self-interest and love of material possessions that, in his view, characterized many white Americans. In contrast, Indians were, he wrote, "generous to the last mouthful of food, fearless of hunger, suffering and death. . . . Not 'to have' but 'to be' was [their] national motto."

Another aspect of white civilization that shocked Eastman was the corruption of its politicians. In Indian culture, leaders received no material benefits for their role. They were therefore not drawn to scheme or make deals in order to keep their position. Moreover, an Indian leader was chosen by the people because he had proven his ability to help them. As soon as he failed to be helpful, another leader would replace him.

Eastman's critical assessment of politicians came, of course, from his unpleasant experiences with the Indian Service. As an agency physician, he had observed first-hand how Indian Service agents exploited their position of power. "Who is this Indian agent, or superintendent, as he is now called?" Eastman wrote in *The Indian Today.* "He is the supreme ruler on the reservation, responsible directly to the Commissioner of Indian Affairs; and all requests or complaints must pass through his office. . . . Too often he has been nothing more than a ward politician of the commonest stamp, whose main purpose is to get all that is coming to him. His salary is small, but there are endless opportunities for graft."

While Eastman may have been bitter because of his own personal experiences—he had been forced to resign twice because of conflicts with Indian agents—his critique of reservation politics was well founded. The Indian service was notorious for its mishandling of Indian complaints. Moreover, the politicians who opted to work for the service tended to be drawn not by a commitment to helping Indians but by the opportunity to make money. Agents could—and often did—indulge in such underhanded activities as illegal trading, stealing from treaty annuities, and land speculation.

Eastman's criticism of whites often channeled into a more focused attack on white–Indian relations. In a reasonable and poised manner, without the slightest trace of rancor, Eastman described how contact with whites perverted and destroyed the Indian way of life. Broken treaties, European diseases, gunpowder, and whiskey— these were the true gifts of civilization. That the whites did not go so far as to exterminate the native peoples of America did not persuade him of their good intentions.

Eastman offered the hypothesis—new for the time, but today accepted by many scholars as having a certain degree of truth—that the U.S. Army purposefully exterminated the buffalo, the Plains Indians' chief source of food, to save itself the trouble of having to slaughter the Indians. Eastman did not mince words in his analysis: "Since it was found cheaper to feed than to fight them, the one-time warriors were corralled upon their reservations and kept alive upon Government rations."

Eastman was at his most critical when discussing the degrading conditions of reservation life. "The Indians of the Northwest came into reservation life reluctantly," he wrote, "very much like a man who has dissipated his large inheritance and is driven out by foreclosure. One morning he awoke to the fact that he must give up his freedom . . . to live in a squalid cabin in the backyard of civilization." The Indians, accustomed to an outdoor life, quickly became prey to tuberculosis, bronchitis, and pneumonia once they were forced indoors into what Eastman described as "overcrowded log cabins." They also suffered from inadequate clothing—usually in the form of surplus U.S. Army blankets—and malnutrition. Rations often consisted of rancid meat—that which the U.S. Army would refuse to eat.

Eastman did not limit himself to complaints. For every wrong he proposed a solution. Agency corruption could be eliminated by replacing the Indian Service Bureau with a team of Indians and whites working together to run the reservation. Health problems could be resolved by teaching the Indians how to cook and clean. And the "physical demoralization, psychological confusion and spiritual apathy" of the Indian could be fought through assimilation efforts. Education and the granting of citizenship would lead the Indian on a new path to freedom.

Eastman's writings made him famous. Invitations came from schools and clubs all over the country asking him to speak on Indian affairs. In 1909, at the height of his popularity, he left the Indian service—his work renaming the Sioux completed—to dedicate most of his time to writing and lecturing. As a young man at Dartmouth, he had already demonstrated his skill as a lecturer when he gave a talk on the French and Indian War at Wellesley College. Now, years later, he proved to be as talented a speaker as he was a writer. His commanding voice and dignified presence made a strong impression on audiences, which greeted him with thunderous applause. Sometimes, to heighten the effect, he gave his lectures

Taking advantage of a rare quiet moment, Elaine Goodale Eastman settles down to read. In addition to editing her husband's manuscripts and managing his business affairs, Eastman's wife helped support her large family by writing numerous novels, poems, and articles.

dressed in the traditional garb of an Indian warrior, replete with eagle-feathered warbonnet, beaded buckskin robe, and tomahawk pipe. Many who saw Eastman speak would later report how struck they were by his charisma and energy.

Elaine Goodale played a major role in her husband's writing and lecturing career. She edited and rewrote most of his books, even though only two bear her name as a coauthor. As she explained to a friend, she took his rough drafts and typed the final versions, "revising, omitting and re-writing as necessary." She also handled most of Eastman's correspondence, communicated with editors, and arranged lecture tours for him. In doing so, she sacrificed some of her commitment to her own writing. Nevertheless, she did find time in between managing her husband's career and raising six children to write seven novels and collections of poetry, numerous articles about Indian life, and a posthumously published autobiography.

In her autobiography, Elaine claimed that she wrote her novels—"potboilers," she called them—to make money. Her husband, despite his rising popularity, still did not earn enough to support his large family. This fact evidently bothered Elaine a great deal. It was she who bore the burden of responsibility for their children while Eastman was away giving lectures.

During this period in his life, it was not only through writing and lecturing that Eastman contributed to the cause of the American Indian—and to his family's income. In 1910, the University of Pennsylvania Museum hired him to collect items from the Ojibwas, the traditional enemy of the Sioux. Eastman traveled through Minnesota and Canada to the camps of his former enemy, accumulating things such as sacred war clubs, bark mats, and beaded artwork. The Ojibwas still lived in the traditional manner of their forebears, gathering berries and rice, hunting, fishing in birch canoes, and tapping sugar from trees. As Eastman camped with them in the dense pine woods near the shores of the great lakes, he remembered how he experienced the world as a child. However, he repressed whatever nostalgia he might have felt. Eastman was always optimistic, and even on this journey he thought as much about the force of nature as he did about how well he was doing in his job accumulating artifacts for the Pennsylvania Museum.

Eastman teaches archery, which he learned as a boy in the Canadian woodlands. Although completely at home in the modern world, he remained deeply attached to the ways of his ancestors.

The trip north gave Eastman an idea. Why not introduce American children to the pleasures of living outdoors? He got in touch with the Boy Scouts of America and inquired whether he could assist with one of their programs. The Boy Scouts of America was a newly formed organization that aimed—like the Boy Scouts of Great Britain—to provide young people with an opportunity to experience nature. It responded to a nationwide nostalgia for the time when the United States had been a mostly undeveloped wilderness. Now that the western frontier was officially closed, and cities and towns had sprung up across the continent, many people felt that a rich part of the American experience was gone. The founders of the Boy Scouts wanted children to know what the United States had been like for their parents and grandparents—the settlers and pioneers who had tamed the wilderness.

The founders of the Boy Scouts were thrilled to have Eastman work for them. He led scouts in the woods and shared with them his considerable knowledge of the

The Eastmans teach a group of campers a Native American dance. Opened in 1915, the couple's School of the Woods became an instant hit with parents eager for their children to experience the outdoors.

outdoors. He also gave lectures to different Boy Scout camps. As usual, Eastman dedicated himself completely to his job and soon rose to the position of camp director. He even wrote a guidebook for the Boy Scouts and Campfire Girls called *Indian Scout Tales* (1914).

Eastman's experiences with the Boy Scouts inspired him to start his own camp. In 1915, he and Elaine opened the School of the Woods in New Hampshire. It was immediately profitable. Camps were just coming into popularity at the time, as urban American parents grew anxious for their children to experience the outdoors. The School of the Woods camp lasted for six years and garnered the Eastman family a steady income. Elaine and Charles ran the camp, while their three oldest daughters—Dora, Irene, and Virginia—acted as counselors. The three girls had inherited their parents' zeal for hard work. Dora had just graduated from college; Irene was training to become a concert soprano; and Virginia was a college student at Wellesley—the same institution at which Eastman had given his first lecture many years back.

During this time, Eastman also participated in the annual Lake Monhonk Conference of Friends of the Indian, a summer event at which leading reformers met to discuss future strategies in helping the Indian assimilate. In April 1911, he and five other educated Indians met together in Columbus, Ohio, to form their own reform group, the first to be led by Indians rather than whites. The idea was to attract members from different tribes who would work collectively to help Indians assimilate. For many years, Eastman was an active member of the Society of American Indians, as this Pan-Indian movement was called. In 1918, he was elected its president.

Perhaps Eastman's most ambitious effort to help his people was his struggle of many years to convince the U.S. government to give the Santee Sioux the money he believed they deserved. After the 1862 Sioux Uprising, the U.S. government voted to break off all its treaties with the Santee Sioux and end payments of annuities. Consequently, the Santee Sioux were forced to fend for themselves, without any restitution for the loss of their land and culture. Eastman, along with many others, argued that this was unfair punishment. Why should all Santee Sioux suffer for an uprising that was led by only a minority of them?

Eastman acted as the Sioux's lawyer from 1884 to 1906. In taking on their difficult case, he revealed his determination to rectify the errors of the past—not only those committed at the expense of his tribe but those that had affected his own life. After all, the Sioux Uprising had broken up Eastman's family and led to his exile in Canada. In restoring the treaties for the Sioux, Eastman might have felt as if he were restoring his own past. Even after his contract as the Sioux's lawyer expired in 1906, he continued to lobby Congress on his own time.

The Eastmans' second daughter, promising concert singer Irene Taluta, died during the nationwide influenza epidemic of 1918. The epidemic, which also killed several campers and counselors at the School of the Woods, contributed to the decline of the camp's popularity.

Another motive may have spurred Eastman to dedicate so many years to the Santee cause: the prospect of making money. As the Santee Sioux's lawyer, he was bound to get 10 percent of all the money they received, up to $250,000. Unfortunately for Eastman, when the case was finally decided by the United States Court of Claims on June 5, 1922—nearly 30 years after he began lobbying— he was no longer the tribe's representative.

Eastman had to petition Congress to receive some remuneration. The Santee Sioux did not want to pay him because the sum would be deducted from their own settlement. Eventually, Congress awarded him $5,000, far less than what he had expected for his years of service.

In the meantime, Eastman's other venture—the camp his family ran in New Hampshire—was not doing well. The 1919 summer season had proven to be a failure. Too few campers came, and the Eastmans could barely handle the costs of running the camp. The decline in enrollment was most likely due to the disastrous conclusion of the previous summer. In 1918, an influenza epidemic spread throughout the country, and areas where many people congregrated—such as theaters, schools, and summer camps—became dens of contagion. Many campers and counselors at the School of the Woods were infected, and some died. One of the victims was Irene Taluta, the Eastmans' second daughter. The Eastmans buried her under a tree at the camp. Three years later, the School of the Woods closed for good.

Irene's death was a terrible blow for Charles Eastman. It was she, out of all his children, whom he often asked to accompany him on his lecture tours. Tall and striking, Irene had inherited her father's commanding stage presence. She had also been an extremely gifted singer, intent on becoming a famous opera star.

This misfortune was not the only difficulty to confront the Eastman family. Charles and Elaine were not getting along—and had not been for some time. Indeed, ever since they first married, rumors had circulated that the two were incompatible.

Whatever the truth, throughout the years, they had grown to resent each other. As Elaine saw it, she had "surrendered" her own promising career as a teacher and supervisor in the Indian service to take care of Charles's career and their children. Staying at home was a shock for this ambitious woman, who had, as a child, been celebrated for her talents. As she wrote, "No, I won't say that the adjustment was easy or that I was never lonely, restless, and haunted by a secret sense of frustration. . . ." She particularly resented being housebound while her husband had the opportunity to travel around the country meeting interesting people. What is more, she suspected Charles of infidelity.

Charles, on his part, found his wife overbearing. According to his nephews, Elaine tried to dominate her husband, particularly in his writing. After a while, Charles resented her editing and rewriting of his books, even though without her influence it is unlikely that he ever would have had them published. Whether Elaine really did a service to her husband in changing his words cannot be known, as none of Eastman's rough drafts exist. However, she can probably be blamed for the romantic turns-of-phrase and cloyingly sentimental passages that riddle Eastman's works and make them seem at times not the work of a former Sioux warrior but of a New England gentleman accustomed to drawing rooms and high tea.

One example suffices. In his autobiography, Eastman refers to himself as "the little Hakadah" who frolics in forests "sweet with the breath of blossoming flowers."

This is the same kind of lofty language that Elaine used in her own works. Brought up in a proper New England home, she had acquired a taste for romantic prose and had evidently imposed her taste on her husband.

A more serious issue was that Elaine and Charles held opposing views about the future of the Indian. While both were dedicated to the project of assimilation, Elaine, unlike Charles, thought it was best for Indians to forget their culture entirely. Elaine's attitude must have angered Charles, especially as he grew closer to his Indian roots. It was his view that Indians could retain and preserve their own culture in the assimilation process.

In his writings, Charles—and, of course, Elaine, his ever-anonymous collaborator—often rhapsodized in favor of interracial marriages. They believed that by marrying into "excellent white families" Indians could boost their position in white civilization, as well as ease intercultural tensions. Their own marriage had been an example to the nation, a symbol of the two cultures coming together. But in August 1921, after 30 years of marriage, Charles and Elaine separated. They did not announce their separation, nor would they ever discuss the reasons that had drawn them apart. Perhaps it was too hard for them to acknowledge to the public that their own personal attempts at assimilation had failed.

11

THE RETURN OF THE GREAT MYSTERY

At the age of 65, Charles Eastman demonstrated the same resolve to confront the hardships of his life as he had at the age of 15, when he left the woods of Canada for the schoolrooms of the United States. Disappointed with the $5,000 he received for his work with the Santee Sioux, he needed to find another job. And so on August 28, 1923, he returned to work for the Bureau of Indian Affairs—the very institution he had so scathingly criticized in his books. He needed the money.

This time Eastman was an Indian inspector—a job unlike any he had ever held for the Indian service. In the past, he had worked on reservations under the supervision of the acting agent. Now the tables had turned. As an Indian inspector, he was responsible for checking the progress of the reservations and investigating any disagreements between agents and Indians. Whereas before he had suffered from the decisions of Indian inspectors, he now made them.

Eastman held this position for three years. During that time, he visited more than 20 reservations, most of them in Oregon and Washington. He occasionally found problems similar to those he had experienced at Pine Ridge and Crow Creek. The Indians at the Mackinac reservation in Michigan, for example, suspected their agent of illegally permitting a lumber company to cut down trees on their land. Eastman investigated the charges and concluded they were unsubstantiated.

Interestingly enough, in most disputes between agents and Indians, Eastman sided with the agent. Perhaps the complaints were unsubstantiated, or perhaps Eastman no longer felt that fighting corruption was worth jeopardizing his own position. One of the times he did criticize an Indian agent—a man named Frank Rogers, head of the Rosebud Agency in South Dakota—Eastman was sternly reprimanded. He had suspended Rogers, who, in Eastman's opinion, had a violent temper and was intolerant of the traditional customs of the Indians. The commissioner of Indian Affairs, Charles Burke, wrote Eastman and told him he had overstepped his authority in suspending Rogers.

During the 1920s, life on the reservations was worse than ever. The efforts that the U.S. government had made to help Indians assimilate seemed to have failed. Indians continued to live in substandard conditions, many in drastic poverty. In 1923, the Secretary of the Interior, Hubert Work, organized a committee to study the situation and to decide what measures had to be taken to improve it. He chose 100 distinguished men, a combination of Indians and whites, to serve on the committee, which was called the Committee of One Hundred. An invitation was naturally extended to Eastman, by then the most famous Indian statesman in the country.

Eastman (far right) attends a party for the 70th birthday of author Mark Twain (seated at another table) in 1905. The nation's most prominent Native American statesman, Eastman often met leading members of white society, encounters he found exhilarating.

Ever since he was a celebrated student at Dartmouth, Eastman had been asked to participate in important national, and even international, conferences. In July 1911, for example, he was invited to represent the North American Indian at the First Universal Races Congress in London. This trip was one of the most memorable events of his life. Not only did he travel across the ocean to a country that, as a child, he had never heard of, but he had the chance to meet with some of the most important politicians and statesmen in the world.

Eastman attends his Dartmouth reunion in 1927 wearing a war-bonnet and buckskin clothing. At this time, he was still active on the lecture circuit.

Throughout his life, Eastman ambitiously pursued—and achieved—a position of power. The Sioux tradition to seek respect and honor in the tribe seemed to have transformed, because of historical necessity, into a desire to rise in white civilization as well. Indeed, out of all the jobs that Eastman held in his lifetime, perhaps it was the role of Indian statesman that most suited him. It was with great pleasure that he would remember, in his memoirs, his meetings with such dignitaries as David Lloyd George, prime minister of England, and Mark Twain, the famous author.

Eastman was satisfied with most of the proposals drafted by the Committee of One Hundred. Like Eastman, the committee recognized the importance of continuing education programs and bettering health conditions on the reservations. It also questioned the earlier policy of trying to eradicate the Indians' native cultures. In the past, the U.S. government had done everything possible to force Indians to give up their traditional identity. For example, at many Indian schools, students were not permitted to speak a word of their native language, and on reservations, many traditional ceremonies and dances were against the law. What the Committee of One Hundred finally realized was that these attempts to strip the Indians of their heritage had only led to greater despair and had done little to help the Indians adjust to white civilization.

As Eastman grew older, he became more and more convinced that "total assimilation" was not a feasible or desirable goal. While he had renounced many aspects of his Sioux heritage, his books and articles revealed that he had never truly rejected the worth of his culture. In fact, by endorsing such activities as the Boy Scouts, he had, in effect, tried to make the Indian way of life become a part of white civilization. His experiences and reflections had distanced him from reformers, such as his wife, Elaine Goodale, who thought "whitewashing" the Indians was the only way to help them.

Eastman's ideas coincided with those that many of his contemporary reformers now held, and his popularity as a lecturer soared. In 1923, he resigned his position as Indian inspector to dedicate his time once again to the lecture circuit. Eastman was nearly 70 years old, but he still arranged to speak before audiences, traveling by train to such cities as New York, Chicago, and Washington, D.C. In 1928, he even accepted an offer from a wealthy woman, Florence Brooks-Aten, to give a two-month lecture tour in England. Interestingly enough, on this occasion, Eastman was not to speak about Indian affairs but about the relationship between the United States and Great Britain. Brooks-Aten had been so impressed with Eastman's efforts to improve

the relationship between Indians and whites that she thought he would do an excellent job promoting Anglo-American friendship.

If Uncheedah were still alive, it might have been hard for her to recognize her grandson, who was now a celebrated figure in the most elite circles of white society. Even though Eastman occasionally dressed as a Sioux warrior when he gave his lectures, he usually sported a starched white shirt and an elegant jacket. He had acquired the sophisticated manners of an upperclass gentleman and was as much at ease consorting with world-renowned diplomats at a five-course dinner as he once had been among deer and antelopes in the woods.

But deep inside Eastman was still Ohiyesa, the boy who had enjoyed the freedom of the wilderness. The more

Eastman and a guide prepare to launch a canoe on Ontario's Rainy River. Despite his success in white society, Eastman felt the continual pull of the woods where he had grown up.

honors and awards he received, the more he must have realized how much he had lost. Perhaps it was during one of the countless formal dinners, or while fox hunting with a group of fine English lords, that Eastman made what must have struck many people as a startling decision. For on his return to the States, he decided he no longer wanted to live in white civilization. He built a cabin for himself in the Canadian woods on the shore of Lake Huron and retired to live in isolation.

Eastman spent the remaining years of his life fishing and hunting in the Canadian woods. The cabin he built had no running water and offered none of the comforts that he had learned to appreciate in the civilized world. But there, in the solitude of the woods, he could once again be Ohiyesa and reconnect with Wankan Tanka, the Great Mystery.

Eastman's return to the woods did not mean he turned his back on white culture. He continued to accept lecture engagements in the United States and to write to his many white friends. Nor did his isolation lead the world to forget him. At the Chicago World's Fair of 1933, the Indian Council Fire nominated him the most accomplished American Indian of his time.

In the seclusion of his hut, Eastman continued to work on different writing projects, although he did not finish or publish any of them—perhaps because Elaine was no longer there to help him. Once in a while, he also treated patients in the nearby towns, bringing into practice the medical knowledge that he had such little occasion to use in his career. During the winter months, Eastman stayed with his son, Ohiyesa II, in Detroit, Michigan. The cold that he had so easily accepted as a child was too much for an old man.

On January 7, 1939, Eastman died at the age of 80. He was buried in an unmarked grave in Detroit. Although

At Lake Minnetonka, Minnesota, in 1927, Eastman shows how he might have looked if he had remained in Santee Sioux society. Although he had felt the need to assimilate into white culture, he also succeeded in casting honor on the memory of his ancestors.

he had lived among white men, he preferred to be buried like an Indian, returning to nature as anonymously as he had come. Besides, no epitaph could have done justice to the complexity of the man who had been Hakadah, Ohiyesa, Charles Eastman, and the Name Giver.

More than a half century after his death, a portrait of Eastman—a gift of his former classmates—still hangs at Dartmouth College. In the picture, he looks quietly into the distance, the hint of fear in his eyes mitigated by the strong tilt of his chin. It is the expression of a Sioux determined to stake out the most dangerous path in the woods—the path to white civilization. As a Sioux leader, it was Eastman's destiny—as it was his forefathers'—to go first and clear the path for his people. Whether he approved of where the path would take them was no matter. He knew they had no choice.

CHRONOLOGY

1858 Born Hadakah near Redwood Falls, Minnesota; mother dies

1862 Santee Sioux rob and murder settlers during the Sioux Uprising; U.S. government forces Santees to leave Minnesota; they flee to Canada; Hadakah earns the name Ohiyesa, meaning "winner"; Many Lightnings, Ohiyesa's father, sentenced to death after the Sioux Uprising

1873 Many Lightnings, now called Jacob Eastman, appears and reunites with Ohiyesa; Ohiyesa moves to Flandreau, South Dakota, with father; Ohiyesa baptized as Charles Alexander Eastman; begins assimilation with white society at a mission school

1883 Enters Dartmouth College in New Hampshire

1887 Graduates from Dartmouth; enters Boston University School of Medicine

1890 Graduates from medical school; becomes government doctor at Pine Ridge Reservation in South Dakota; treats victims of Wounded Knee massacre

1891 Marries Elaine Goodale; moves to St. Paul, Minnesota; starts medical practice; begins to write memoirs

1894 Becomes traveling organizer for the Young Men's Christian Association (YMCA); establishes 43 YMCA chapters for Native Americans

1899 Works as agent for the Carlisle School in Pennsylvania, helping Native American children adjust to white culture

1902 Takes job as agency physician at the Crow Creek Reservation in South Dakota

1903 Appointed "Name Giver" for the entire Sioux nation; gives short English names to more than 25,000 Sioux

1915 Opens the School of the Woods, a New Hampshire summer camp

1918 Elected president of the Society for American Indians; loses daughter Irene to influenza epidemic

1921 Separates from Elaine Goodale Eastman after 30 years of marriage

1923 Becomes inspector for the U.S. Indian Service; joins the Committee of One Hundred—formed to improve the lives of Native Americans

1939 Dies in Detroit, Michigan, home of his son, Ohiyesa II

FURTHER READING

Eastman, Charles. *From the Deep Woods to Civilization: Chapters in the Autobiography of an Indian.* Boston: Little, Brown, 1916.

———*Indian Boyhood.* New York: Dover Publications, 1902.

———*Indian Heroes and Great Chieftains.* Boston: Little, Brown, 1918.

———*Indian Scout Talks: A Guide for Boy Scouts and Camp Fire Girls.* Boston: Little, Brown, 1914.

——— *The Indian Today: The Past and Future of the First American.* Garden City: Doubleday, Page, 1915.

———*Red Hunters and the Animal People.* New York: Harper and Brothers, 1904.

Eastman, Mary. *Dahcotah; or, Life and Legends of the Sioux Around Fort Snelling.* New York: Ayer, 1849.

Graber, Kay, ed. *Sister to the Sioux: The Memoirs of Elaine Goodale Eastman, 1885–91.* Lincoln: University of Nebraska Press, 1978.

Lee, Betsy. *Charles Eastman.* Minneapolis: Dillon Press, 1979.

Mooney, James. *The Ghost-Dance Religion and the Sioux Outbreak of 1890.* Chicago: University of Chicago Press, 1965.

Utley, Robert. *The Last Days of the Sioux Nation.* New Haven: Yale University Press, 1963.

INDEX

PICTURE CREDITS

KARIN LUISA BADT holds a B.A. in creative writing from Brown University and a Ph.D. in comparative literature from the University of Chicago. This is her eighth book for young readers.

W. DAVID BAIRD is the Howard A. White Professor of History at Pepperdine University in Malibu, California. He holds a Ph.D. from the University of Oklahoma and was formerly on the faculty of history at the University of Arkansas, Fayetteville, and Oklahoma State University. He has served as president of both the Western History Association, a professional organization, and Phi Alpha Theta, the international honor society for students of history. Dr. Baird is also the author of *The Quapaw Indians: A History of the Downstream People* and *Peter Pitchlynn: Chief of the Choctaws* and the editor of *A Creek Warrior of the Confederacy: The Autobiography of Chief G. W. Grayson.*